TOUGH TIMES

WHEN THE MONEY DOESN'T LOVE US

Tough Times

When the money doesn't love us

Edited by John B. Lee

Black Moss Press
2010

Library and Archives Canada Cataloguing in Publication

Tough times : when the money doesn't love us / edited by John B. Lee.

ISBN 978-0-88753-470-6

I. Lee, John B., 1951-

PS8233.T68 2010 C810.8 C2010-905364-8

Cover photographs by Marty Gervais
Design by Karen Veryle Monck

Black Moss Press is published at 2450 Byng Road, Windsor, Ontario, Canada N8W 3E8. Black Moss books are distributed in Canada and the U.S. by LitDistco. All orders should be directed there.

Black Moss can be contacted on its website at www.blackmosspress.com.

Black Moss acknowledges the generous support for its publishing program from The Canada Council for the Arts and The Ontario Arts Council.

Le Conseil des Arts du Canada | The Canada Council for the Arts

ONTARIO ARTS COUNCIL
CONSEIL DES ARTS DE L'ONTARIO

Printed in Canada

I have been through some terrible things in my life,
some of them actually happened.
– Mark Twain

In their youth both Herder and Schiller intended
to study as surgeons, but Destiny said:
"No, there are deeper wounds than those of the body,
– heal the deeper!" and they wrote.
– Jean Paul Richter, writer (1763-1825)

Table of Contents

4

5

6

Preface: One Wet Eye on the Money

John B. Lee

In the autumn of 2008, my uncle and mother sold the home farm that had been in the Lee family for five generations. This major financial transaction involved the exchange of fertile land for a substantial sum of money made possible by the availability of credit. The purchaser of the land was deemed a good risk by the bank and a worthy guardian of the Lee legacy by the vendors.

A central tenet of my paternal grandfather's rural creed had been based upon the tiller of the earth's commitment to preservation of topsoil and improvement of arable land. After all, the earth of the father becomes the soil of the son. And the family that bought our land was a similar champion of this creed.

So, the painful surrender of proprietorship became a necessary sacrifice due to the crisis of old age and the reality that no one in the Lee clan was either interested in or capable of carrying on the farming of the land. There were no more farmers with farming in their blood and sufficient capital to carry on the consanguinity of Leeland Farms.

This transition did not occur without pain and conflict within the family. Some of those who knew the need to sell did not share the conviction of the necessity to sell. Some of those peripheral to the transaction inveigled themselves in ways destructive to the good will of those more directly involved in assisting the essential parties in the execution of transfer of ownership. Indeed, there were bitter words and broken bonds.

Quite often over the course of this painful transition, my mother, half-owner of this widow's land, could be heard to lament, "Money is the root of all evil."

My uncle, whose idea it was that the time had come to sell, became an ear to bend, and I, as sole confidant of both parties, came to be seen in the eyes of some as a source of shame. Lies got legs, relatives cursed my name, and I became a quiet victim of mendacity, distrust, vituperation, and undeserved opprobrium. Nonetheless, the sale went through, the money appeared in the private accounts of Uncle and Mother, and then the world of money collapsed on a global scale. Moneylenders lost the money to lend.

This is an entirely accidental vindication of an urgent event. The sale of the farm had been urgent due to age and failing health on the part of the joint owners. It had become possible because both parties saw the necessity and the possibility of the sale. The sale of the land was an important event not only because of the considerable monetary value of the property, but more importantly because of the generations of the Lees who had identified themselves with the family legacy directly connected to the family farm. Leeland Farms that had been a source of family pride had briefly become a source of family conflict.

In December of the year of the sale of Leeland Farms the global economy collapsed. International banks failed. The stock market crashed. People lost their life savings. The auto industry went into crisis. Unemployment soared in cities like Windsor and Oshawa where the car industry had once thrived and autoworkers had prospered. Housing values plunged. In the United States, president Obama committed over a trillion dollars to the shoring up of the financial institutions. The famous black bull of Wall Street vanished and Merrill Lynch expired. Suddenly, those who had resisted the sale of the farm were counting their blessings.

I sometimes wish away the wealth of relatives because I'm sure they never really know whether or not those concerned for their welfare in old age do not have one wet eye on the money. This book, *Tough Times*, deals with painful moments in the lives of writers. Sometimes, there is no obvious relationship between the tale being told herein and the collapse of 2008 and the subsequent sorrow of 2009. Sometimes the relationship is obvious and direct. Whatever the case, every piece herein makes a connection between writing and healing. Literature yearns for a world where even those with one wet eye on the money know the true value of caring has nothing to do with filthy lucre.

1

The Boy Who Ate Dragonflies

Dylan Lee

Two years ago, the boy who ate dragonflies sat in my room on the first day of class and wept.

"I don't like this damn school"

"Okay," I said.

"I never see my father."

His eyes dance light off the desktop. They don't hold still for a second. Behind the transparent lens of his plastic-frame glasses, they move in torn, contemporaneous light.

He is wearing his winter uniform. A permanent-pressed line stiffens his mother-ironed gray slacks. In sharp contrast to his fastidious classmates, a blue necktie he refuses to tighten hangs loose exposing the glassy pearl of an unfastened top button of his white shirt revealing a faded purple tee worn underneath. To the left side of the room, three seats from the back, four from the front, next to a row of windows he sits face out to the tree-lined path running three floors below.

Standing behind the podium at the front of the room, I cannot read his nametag. The chick-yellow embroidery of affricate syllables melts into the white tag making it illegible. At this angle and from this distance, it appears as a mere dusting of turmeric and saffron in sugar.

The standard-issue blue blazer bought last year is four inches short in the arm. The banderole of willowy wrist and hand droop from the front edge of his desk. His shoulders choke inside the narrow blue poly viscose-andcotton blend back. His head is drawn into his shoulders giving him the hunched appearance of a scoliosis sufferer.

He must be poor. Most of the other formerly small kids have bought new jackets before the start of semester. The wilier boys with parents who don't mind or don't know any better walk around wearing the oversized coats of former first year giants. They've lost their names by so doing. Now each class has one less Ji-Su and one more Seok-Hwan, one more Dong-Gyu. Identities absorbed into paint and paper and floorboard. My students all go by the name of someone who went before them like a smattering of clerical errors at a conference of strangers.

Now, staring out the window—more like staring *at* the window—the reflection *in* the glass—he refuses to look me in the eye. The first rule of proper American-style conversation: look one another in the eye. I make note of his failure to do so in my ledger. We'll have to work on this together.

"What does your father do? I mean, what is his job?"

I adjust my meaning through this quick and reflexive repetition learned after three years of ESL teaching. Three years wherein I have had to capture student interest and thereby force them to understand my meaning. This kid doesn't want engagement. He doesn't wish to talk. My importuning seems indelicate. I cannot even tell if he is listening.

He shifts his glance from the window and aims his attention at the floor seeming to take note of a sheet of recycled-gray paper fallen at his feet, then speaks.

"He works fourteen hours a day in an office and then drives a cab twelve hours a night."

The 24 hours in a day math error he's made doesn't dawn on him. But no one in the room is willing to challenge him on this.

• • •

In the winter, the Han River flows as a steel-gray bifurcation cutting through the two great halves of Seoul. In the hot wet sultry days of summer it swells into a torrent between its banks. I've read about buses washing past as it crests in flash floods. I've seen the rushing waters choked with brown silt eroded from the mountains as I stared from the wet windows of a subway car. I've witnessed the rise and fall of the great river suffering seasonal undulations. I've watched it flashing through the glass of my television filmed by helicopter journalists. In my weekly migration into the city I realize I am ten years too late. I did not experience the makeshift tarpaulin tent guyed in yellow rope erected by that boy's destitute father on the edge of Seoul's great Han River.

• • •

The boy who ate dragonflies
darts through chest-high grass
wild flax
pale brown
parched and arid
with autumn.

Behind his sister.

Ten years later
she
would arrive
as a student teacher
at my school
wearing a white
sleeveless summer dress

She who one year
studied in college
while her recalcitrant brother
sat in my classroom

She is four years older
much taller than
the boy who ate dragonflies

Her arms
locked at the elbows
and mop-handle thin
slice through
this stiff river hair

The grass
rights itself
in her passing
like stiff ribs
released from a bear hug
like malleable
elastic frog bones
like cloth-draped wings

of a monocoque plane
slicing through cloud
and reconstituting
in the thermal drag
of its stir

Closed fisted.
Closed eyes
looking out
the sting of her flesh.
Threshing:
amber stalks of grass
in neat-armed flail
in plaster-stiff movement.

• • •

The butterfly net is taut
pulled open by air
like delicate rainbow water
of soap-bubble membrane
growing through the halo
of a child's breath.

Then they catch wings.
They are both hungry
since their father
lost
work
car
home

Entomologists of the gut these days
they press their delicate captured specimens
into palatial memory
carving in each entry
like an acid-etched
bronze plate

along with minnow
hand fished
and fast swallowed
the ones that infected them with parasitemia
their book is quickly filled

They singe off
wings
legs flare
for a moment
like birch bark
in a campfire

the yellow-orange flame
of the lighter
whips out
in harvest air
when they snap
the striker
it brands
their thumbs

On the bike path
near the tent
they walk slowly back

they don’t like to
tell their mother
how hungry
they are

Breakfast, Lunch, Dinner
and Life Outside of the World

John B. Lee

"the poor always ye have with you"

–John 12, 8

Breakfast

Consider the case of a special education teacher in a small inner-city elementary school. The parent-teacher council decided to run a breakfast program to serve the needs of the children and to raise funds for school necessities. The school budget, for example, was unable to provide paper towel and soap to supply the student washrooms for the remainder of the year.

The council successfully acquired food donated at no cost to the school. Volunteers prepared and served the breakfast. The organization charged 25 cents per student and the teachers encouraged universal participation on the part of their classes.

In the special education class one the most needy students remained silent when everyone else paid the quarter required for participation. The teacher approached the student in question and said, "You should participate in this program. You need pay only 25 cents for a hearty breakfast, a great way to start your day. Come to school early, join your friends, and we'll serve up a wonderful meal."

"I can't, Miss."

"And why not?"

"My mother doesn't have 25 cents, Miss."

The teacher returned to her desk. Lesson learned.

Lunch*

A Russian oil tycoon and owner of a football club in the company of another man and his son and three business partners stopped over for lunch at a restaurant in New York City.

It became obvious immediately that the high quality of food and service would take priority over cost. The tycoon began his dinner with carpaccio with white truffles followed by Milan lamb with pasta and Parmesan. For dessert he tried delicious tiramisu. They were all drinking the best champagne and the most expensive wine. To the waiter they looked no different from any typical New York tourists.

Drinks included two bottles of Chateau Petrus, three bottles of La Tache Romanee Conti pinot noir and two 1.5 litre bottles Cristal Rose champagne at $5,000 per bottle.

The drinks alone came to $35,000. One of the teetotallers in the party was drinking $16 mineral water.

The Russian's face remained unchanged when he saw the bill. He inquired only if the service was included. The owner of the restaurant presented the extravagant diner with a soccer ball as a memento for being a special client, and in jest, suggested perhaps he might consider buying the Yankees.

The cost for 1 hour and 18 minute lunch came to $47,000. Although the bill included 20% tip, they gave the waiter an additional $5,000 in cash.

In total they spent $52,000 for lunch.

**based upon a true story widely disseminated on the internet*

Dinner

Manuel is a good man. A father of three sons, he does his best by his children. His eldest son is an ophthalmologist who makes his money as a visual artist. His youngest child is a boy just now reaching school age. His middle son is a fifth-year medical student studying in Holguín.

One evening this middle child turned up at his doorway hungry, hot and tired. Hungry because he does not have the money for a meal. Hot because his is a torpid nation without air conditioning for the citizens. Tired because he is ground down by his circumstances and the constant need to study.

In his country, the educated classes often make far less in a month than a taxi driver, a waiter in a restaurant, or a maid turning beds in tourist hotel make in a single day of tips. This is an upside-down pyramid of an economy.

If asked, Manuel might say, with a laugh, as he did recently, "My country does not have an economy. My country is outside of the world."

He told his son to go into the newly constructed bathroom and take a bath while he prepared dinner. "Actually, to be truthful, I shared my meagre dinner with my much discouraged son," he said.

Fresh from the bath, with a belly full of his father's cooking, he asked without a hint of irony, "Dad. When will this revolution be over?"

"I sent him on his way. Fed. Clean. I pray for him," he said. "I pray for him. We all want a better life for our children, don't we?"

"Indeed, we do." I might have said. Instead, I said nothing. Instead, I thought of our common world, and I too wished for a world outside of this one.

Fine Foods

Bernice Lever

Finally, I can use Aunt Kay's bulging scribbler of scraps of yellowing, browning newspaper. In the '30s (maybe earlier as a young bride), she snipped out "Helpful Hints" and "Economic Recipes". These she glued (no scotch taped then) to both sides until her pages became obese. Many handwritten treasures swapped from friends and family were included. Who could afford a cookbook?

Now, I am looking forward to "Bread Crumb Drops" made from crushed dried crusts and other carbo, bits mixed with bacon fat (drippings always hoarded), beaten egg (people kept chickens), a little flour and a good dusting of cinnamon. "Quick bakers, Hot oven." One of my childhood favourites, like the many mother magically produced in the Ration Days of WWII. During sugar shortages, she spooned molasses or caramel syrup from a tin bucket.

Maybe now is the time for 'block or apartment parties' to share recipes for vegetarian meals, even decide who has a cool basement fro cold storage of root vegetables. Enjoy bean or potato & onion soup—without even saying the "V" word. Dried and jarred foods last for years without refrigeration and its electricity costs. Herb and salad greens in window pots will enliven one's bare rooms. What have you to barter in goods or services for food? Can you fish or breed rabbits?

Luckily, in 2009, many people have enough clothes for a decade. Soon the patched and faded office trousers can vie with the patched and faded designer jeans. Has the "in crowd" been getting us ready for clothing swaps? People will learn to darn socks and mend underwear. Some already know how to knit and sew. Creativity returns!

Room in one's closets will be welcomed as more and more people share housing. Even the art of conversation, perhaps storytelling will be revived. The loneliness of one person per TV or computer screen will disappear. People beginning to laugh as they sip their chosen home brew: potato champagne or wild-berry wine.

People do get creative when they don't have credit cards, let alone ready cash, to instantly gratify their every whim. This Depression could reduce addictive cravings, while teaching the joys of anticipation. It will certainly slow down our wastefulness of natural resources. Our First Nations of each region of every continent know what is provided free by Nature. This abused earth has much to offer; just listen to the oral history from past generations. Survivors will learn from past upheavals.

Google cannot find you crisp spring chickweed or baby dandelion leaves for salads or birch-bark tea for vitamin C, or thousands of other foods and herb remedies. So, share recipes and food with folktales as you develop new friendships in this Depression. "Prayer is free." There is abundance to feed the body, mind and spirit.

The Man Who Made Hope

John B. Lee

Esperanza in Spanish
the word for hope
gives name
to this green gift
the insect made from grass
woven into the living shape
I held
in my open hand
as I sat
turning over the fire
the suckling we were roasting
to share at a later meal
and my clothing
spiced with smoke
remembers this burning hour
this early afternoon
we watched the ancient egrets
in flight
the white memory
of their old going
etched in the bent-winged water

and now
the blackened body
of that ornamental blade
rattled silent, sits
on my desk

a windless remnant of a Cuban glade
folded by the man
who made hope
from the locus of one green day
under the lost blue sky
of his land
his hope

2

A Defence of Poetry

Chris Faiers

Rich In Spirit, Poor In Pocketbook: Entering the Poets' Paradigm

Most fellow poets I've known have been rich in spirit, but poor in pocketbook. With this global financial collapse, large portions of the rest of the population will be forced to consider the economic conditions many poets consider normal, even ideal.

As I prepared to start this brief essay, I received my daily email from poet Michael Zizis. It was a quote by Robert Graves, "There's no money in poetry, but then there's no poetry in money, either."

Too true. This is the reality most poets accept and live by. I remember when I was starting my small literary press three decades ago. Two poets who were beginning to establish credible reputations decided to become lawyers. At the time, being incredibly naive, I couldn't fathom how two such talented wordsmiths could choose this path in life. Why be a financially secure lawyer, and a respected member of society, when you could be an impoverished poet looked down upon by a capitalist society which worships money, power, success and consumerism?

Scientists are now describing an 'empathy gene'. When I was a hard-core lefty, my comrades and I used to think right wingers were stupid. Decades have proven this untrue. But maybe the explanation of a missing empathy gene does explain the attitudes and behaviour of most of our political leaders (the ultimate oxymoron).

Perhaps there is a yet-undiscovered 'poet gene' which leads some down the garden path of poverty, misunderstood empathy, and little or no public recognition, but which does cultivate a richness of the mind and spirit. Those strange creatures with this genetic anomaly are POETS!

In 1821 Percy Bysse Shelley concluded his "A Defence of Poetry" with the sentence, "Poets are the unacknowledged legislators of the world". We are not lawyers, nor politicians, and we often consciously choose to live in conditions normal people would rightly consider appalling. But generation after generation of new poets are born, and continue to choose this life path.

The richness of spirit experienced by all poets, and beautifully expressed by some, is life enough for those with a true understanding of the wonder of this human existence. I think of William and Dorothy Wordsworth wandering the English Lake District, tiny Dove Cottage more than sufficient refuge from the not-so-rugged wildness of their domain.

Closer to home, I think of Jim Larwill, living year round in his cottage lacking indoor plumbing, content to watch the seasons change around his small lake in rural Quebec.

We daydream of the 'great generation' of Canadian poets, Milton Acorn sitting on a sand dune by the shores of his native Prince Edward Island. Al and Eurithe Purdy cozied to Roblin Lake, hidden even from public acclaim in the pioneer hamlet of Ameliasburgh.

Simple lives on the surface, but lives more fully lived,

more deeply understood and in tune with the phases of the moon, the length of winters, the breezes of spring, the flowers and the falling leaves. These are ecologically valid ways to live. No SUVs to carve through downtown traffic. A jug of homemade wine, a pail of fresh water from the lake, and thou beside me in the Canadian wilderness, perhaps.

Cliched, yes. A role model for a less money-oriented future society, which has suddenly, impossibly become NOW. Hopefully.

We can whine and complain about our dwindled mutual funds, our inability to afford a new car this year, or the loss of our ability to daily support the local trendy cafe. Or we can learn to live like our role model poets, the unacknowledged legislators, who have been thriving on bucolic, back-to-the-land lifestyles since we shared our first dens with moneyless wolf brethren.

Rich in spirit, poor in pocketbook. The new paradigm is here, become free to enjoy it.

POETRY POWER! It's the new paradigm.

Poetry Sales in Times like These

Antony Di Nardo

Poetry sales, I've learned, have been brisk at *Librairie Antoine* here on Hamra, though "brisk" may be too strong a word and likely creates the wrong impression. It might be more prudent to say, especially in these times of economic hardship when one would expect caution to prevail, that poetry sales, unlike those of the other genres on the bookstore shelves, have not fallen. There is no other explanation, it seems, for this peculiar phenomenon, for this sustained run on books of poetry when poetry usually accounts for less than 1% of total book sales at this, and likely any of the bookstores on the planet, other than to point the finger at the sudden economic slump that has devastated the banking sector and taken the bottom out of public and private investments pushing the markets to the brink of a global depression. Despite the Dow Jones gloom, poetry sales, as a percentage of total bookstore receipts, have more than doubled at Antoine's, regarded by most standards as the city's barometer for what's hot and what's not in books. Is poetry, then, a salve for market depression paranoia? Does poetry really divert the spirits of those troubled by money matters, drawing attention away from the mundane realities of quotidian life in the marketplace to a loftier realm of reflection and contemplation in a yet-to-be-repossessed leather armchair? Can poetry ever be, like art in gilded frames hung on pampered walls, a safe investment in times of uncertainty? Unlikely.

We should not discount, however, that men and women have in difficult times turned to literature, and poetry in particular, for solace and distraction. A case in point is the poetry of Auden, that hero of the thirties' left, and that of Frost, two writers of some repute whose work during the Great Depression, while reflective of the harsh realities and social inequities of the times, was illuminated by the latent hope of humanity's moral righteousness and existential quest, and captured, as they say, the public imagination. They sold poetry by the armload. Seating space at reading venues where these poets enjoyed top billing had to be steadily increased, their popularity rising as the country's solvency declined. Frost's definition of poetry as a "momentary stay against confusion" declared the poet's imagination as a possible anchor in a sea of social and cultural change. There was also a steadily growing audience back then for radio poetry, as evidenced by Tom Malone on NBC and Tony Wons on CBS whose readings spanned the airwaves and the psyche of America. The NBC broadcast, "Between the Bookends," consisted of 15 minutes of daily poetry and attracted thousands of listeners to their tube-driven Electrohomes and RCAs. A 1935 issue of *Newsweek* reported that Tom Malone, in his first year on the air, received the most fan mail of any un-sponsored broadcast in America, upwards of 20,000 pieces of fan letters in a month.

Also, witness the Beat poets of the fifties and early sixties who attracted almost as much attention for being the iconoclasts of the decade as the Soviets who were launching Sputnik into space, an event that placed America in the grip of national fear, so powerful was the impulse to resist the status of becoming second-best and risking emasculation by its cold-war foe. There is a charming b&w

photo of Allen Ginsberg, circa 1960, reading in Washington Square Park with a throng of admirers and listeners surrounding him, some perched in the cradling boughs of the leafy trees, and hanging, evidently, on his every word. The limits of photography captures only several hundreds at this public reading, but our imaginations allow us to assume there were thousands beyond the fringes of the frame, thousands delivered to the spectacle of poetry. This, lest we forget, at a time when one would have expected fallout shelter drills to draw far greater crowds and outnumbering any poetry reading. And only recently, after the attack on the Twin Towers, Don DeLillo in his novel, *Falling Man*, imagined New Yorkers turning to poetry in the days that followed. "People read poems," he wrote. "People I know, they read poetry to ease the shock and pain, give them a kind of space, something beautiful in language."

More remarkable, perhaps, is the little known poetry-phenom that was A.J. McClerk, a French-Canadian with an Irish mother who had changed his name from Alfred Leclerc when he hit the rails in the early thirties and took his prodigious versifying across the country, singing paeans to the hobo's life or reciting from his epic on a six-course meal, suffused with such palpable imagery, as legend has it, that no listener in the audience ever left the scene on an empty stomach. Unfortunately, there's little of his work that survives in print. A master of memorization, his poetry rested comfortably on the bedroll of his wanderlust and would waken whenever McClerk felt a need to enliven a sullen gathering of restless travellers or an uneasy scrabble of men waiting in the rain for a day's worth of labour. He'd pass the hat for pennies on such occasions, fully expecting to come up empty, and he usually did, but never without several well-placed words of appreciation and gratitude. He was thin and gaunt, practically emaciated: unsurprisingly, since most of the people in his audiences would also fit that description. But when reciting his verse from the back of a pick-up or the edge of a boxcar, he appeared almost skeletal, a mere speck of a man—some said spectre—like a ghost that materialized only when he spoke. His poetry at its best lifted spirits, raised the downcast out of their gloom, transcended the mundane plight of homelessness and vagabondery that the desperate and the disillusioned in his ranks suffered quietly enough. It gave them "a kind of space, something beautiful in language," as DeLillo wrote, to rescue them from themselves. Though prone to grand Victorian sweeps of verse, typical of the Canadiana of the times, his work was grounded in the real, the shocks and tumbles of lived experience, and often not without moments of musical reverie, as in this fragment from a longer work known as "The Cattle Riders:"

We were happiest in the glowing morn, among the gleaming grass,
To wander as we wandered many a mile,
And blow the cool tobacco cloud, and watch the white wreaths pass,
Sitting loosely in the saddle all the while.
We were happiest amid the woods, when we spied the rancher's roofs,
To wheel the wild scrub cattle at the yard,
With a running fire of snapping whips and fiery run of hoofs:
O! the hardest day was never then too hard!

My great-uncle, who was fortunate to keep his job at CP Rail during that Depression and had more than a passing acquaintance with the rail jockeys and their stories, praised McClerk's gift as raconteur and crowd-pleaser, remembering how he could turn the line of a poem just so, his rhythms and his phrasing just so, and all of this, my uncle would proudly say, "without a gee-tar or a microphony." History may not have enshrined McClerk with the wit and homespun wisdom of a Will Rogers, but his natural command of the poet's medium and the savour of his words drew his fair share of admiring crowds north of the border. That other Canadian poet, Bliss Carman, may well have been thinking of his younger contemporary when he wrote these unfortunate couplets:

With only another league to wend;
And two brown arms at the journey's end!

These are the joys of the open road—
For him who travels without a load.

McClerk's poetry was born in and out of troubled times. It embodied a life on the rails and the travails of acknowledging a seemingly endless road of hardships that only a few well-placed words could assuage. When one considers the crowds that would flock to hear McClerk recite, at times several hundred hopelessly hopeful souls in attendance either in a small southern Ontario town or prairie railroad yard, one is struck by how great the need for poetry must have been back then to ease a weary mind, calm a restless spirit, or just simply pass the time.

So is it any wonder that poetry sales have not met the same fate as other genres at Antoine's in today's escalating global recessionary-deflationary depression? Or have they?

Let's consider another side of this inflated coin. (Or is it deflated now?) Ever ask yourself why poetry in the 21st century ranks the lowest of all bookstore sales? Why Antoine's margins have poetry at less than 1% of total receipts? The answer is simple. Because poetry is a hard sell. Period. Few people read it. End of discussion. It's a well-known fact that, save for those who turn to it "to ease the shock and pain," the major consumers of poetry are poets themselves. The accusation is legion: poets in the post-modern, post-modem era write only for other poets. It's mostly poets who buy poetry, and, though their numbers are growing, there aren't that many of them. Imagine the state of the publishing world if only novelists bought books of fiction. You could count on one or two hands the number of racks in the fiction section—still, no doubt, a sight more than the poetry shelf. There'd be busloads of aimless, unemployed critics circling the boulevards of broken dreams. Bookstores would be mostly coffee shops. And what need would we have for the weekend paper's ubiquitous bestseller list? The towers of the publishing world would collapse.

In the United States, the industry standard for a book of poems comes in at about 2000 copies. A print run for a collection of poetry in Canada is usually 500 copies, at best 750. Poets are paid in copies of their own books, not dollars. Other than sales of fat anthologies and course-listed collections for university credits, poetry has little or no popular appeal. Exceptions, of course, are the rule. Leonard Cohen has not done too badly. The former American poet laureate, Billy Collins, has reached a semi-mass market public with sales numbering over half a million copies according to his publisher. Not bad for a poet and academic. However, for the average poet, eager to autograph the oeuvre of a lifetime, book sales at a reading, which are usually sparsely attended, or at literary festivals where writers often outnumber readers, fare far better than in bookstores. Which goes to show the paucity of volumes on the poetry shelf that actually make it out the front door.

But these stats do little to answer our question: why this sudden surge in the percentage of poetry sales at Antoine's? To put it simply, and to echo a well-worn slogan, it's the economy, stupid! Allow me to illustrate.

As faithful as poets may be to poetry, and as well stocked as their toolboxes may be with the latest in synonyms and metaphors, truth is they have very little money. Money in a poet's savings account is, in literary circles, the equivalent of military intelligence—an oxymoron. Money in a poet's grip is tantamount to the proverbial water in a sieve and, unless Aunt Penelope leaves a handsome inheritance, his consumer patterns seldom change. Versified, a poet's spending habits go something like this:

Coffee, wine
And pay the rent;
Coffee, wine
(Get laid) and pay the rent;
Some for books

And these good looks,
Oh shit! the money's spent.

It's a kind of *a-b, a-b, c-c, b* of lyrical accounting.

Poets, according to an informal poll, maintain a low-budget book-purchasing regimen of less than half a dozen volumes per year, preferring to borrow each other's photocopied pages rather than spend good cash on one of those hard-to-reach pencil-thin paperback they find at the rear of a bookstore. Should a poet sell a poem or two to a journal—oh, the unvarnished joy, the unabashed relief of not receiving yet another rejection note!—she reels in a cheque of barely 50 bucks or so, and will likely use it to splurge on a book of poems, a G-G winner perhaps, and a second-hand scarf.

No, sales, we could argue, aren't really up at all at Antoine's—they've just stayed the same. Poets have no money. What were we thinking? The fact of the matter is—and to put this exceptional market economy anomaly to rest—the reality of bookstore accounting at Antoine's is such that, because of this depression we're in, it's the other book sales that are down, giving the *illusion* that poetry sales are up, percentage wise, that is, when in truth, they haven't budged. And therein resides the real stuff of poetry's resilience, regardless of the stock-ticker-buffeting that bookstores and the economy must endure. Poetry survives on the illusory, dwells in the region of invention, of shadow-play and ambiguity. With time and experience so compressed in a few choice words drawn from the hard-core galaxies of the metaphor and its satellites, poetry creates its own realities with its own sets of rules, and is entirely founded on the knowledge that, as one poet said, it will never change the world and will surely never repair the economic hard-times we face. But survive it, it will, no matter its bookstore sales. It lives in its articulation, as poets so well know, descanting aches and pains and hunger, beauty and anguish, happiness and love, longing and shortfalls, triumphs and failures, the beaten path and the road less travelled, the horrific, the subtle, the leap of faith, fallen towers and the names of things, the dank, the dangerous, the shape of the sky, the sweep of an ocean, the heightened lyric of the absurd and the clarity of the surreal. And all other sorts of privileged binaries and mismatched pairs. It survives its own anarchy, exists in a world where makers are self-licensed to make it up. In just a few lines. Compressed. Contained. In a pencil-thin paperback. On the back shelf. Hard to reach. But attainable. Oh, so attainable. Even in troubled times.

A Writer's Life in Three Minutes

Shane Jospeh

I once attended a writers' conference in San Francisco where authors were given an opportunity to speed-date with literary agents. Each author had three minutes to make his pitch. At first, I thought that this exercise was trivializing the novel I had worked on for six years—how dare they ask me to boil it down to three minutes? My indignation was compounded when the agents informed the authors that they in turn had only 30 seconds to pitch the chosen manuscripts to their publishers before final selections were made.

I was surprised at how packed this conference was: 400 writers—make that, wannabe writers. Stock markets around the world had imploded, but there was no recession inside here; as unemployment lines climbed the hills of this beautiful city, amateur writers (perhaps some of them were from those very lines outside) had shown up in force at the conference centre, in the hope of landing that dream contract and living forever after isolated from the dullards of society, with royalty cheques and celebrity-appearance invitations pouring in. And I had thought that Canada was the only country inhabited with more writers than readers!

I practised my pitch in my lonely hotel room, and however hard I tried, I was still running well over ten minutes. After all, I had to tell them how much I had sweated, how many rejection slips I had earned, show them the scars. They had to feel my pain, before I told them what my book was all about. And then I had to launch into all the juicy bits of my novel... Three minutes? Duh!

On the big day, I humbly stood in line behind my fellow scribblers, feeling as if I was going to the gallows. There were about ten different lines snaking about the room, each destined for a literary agent. Some agents looked bored, others were trying to focus above the nervous chatter, and others seemed genuinely interested in finding a needle in this haystack of dreams about to land on them. I had my script prepared—I had reluctantly cut it down to three minutes, feeling that my best bytes had been sacrificed, like I had given up my wife, first born and dog all in a fell swoop of my editing pen. Three minutes!

When my turn came, I did all the wrong things, naturally. I made no eye contact, did not relax, I just stuck to my script and rattled away. There were only three minutes, damn it—I was not going to waste them on chit chat. I knew I had blown it when the bell rang, even though the kindly agent asked me to send in a sample of my work. I thought she was being polite.

Before I got to the next table, I re-grouped. This was not how I had planned things. What was the agent buying? Me—that was all I had to sell! The novel was incidental; it had come out of a complex set of fears, imagination, ambition and experience called "Me, Inc." That was what I was selling. I threw out my script. Blast it, I had worked on this novel for six years, I should be able to talk it through back to front. I took a sip of water from my bottle and sat down in front of the next agent. I was beaming with revelation.

I saw three other agents during the remainder of that session, and my performance only improved each time.

I opened myself up for them to see Me, Inc: what I had written, and why, and what new contribution I had to make to the literary canon already out in the universe. And surely, I told myself and them, if I hadn't made a contribution, then I did not deserve to be there. Every three-minute stint thereafter, was sacred. I blotted out the outside noise, reaching into myself, facing my Maker as it were, and rendered an account of what the years in my life had produced. Place, protagonist and problem: that's all that mattered and I stuck to them. In three minutes! I felt good.

Those three agents also asked me to submit sample material in the end. I felt that the three minute segments were the best ones that I have experienced in my life as a writer. Yes, it is possible to distil a life down to three minutes, I realized, just as it is possible to blow it out into a five hundred page novel or a five thousand word short story—that demonstrates the skill, and is the job, of the writer.

It's been a long time since I returned from that conference. Some agents responded, "....unfortunately, we are unable..." Others did not bother. And I am hoping that all of them do not reply, because I can then cling to the hope that somewhere out there, someone is still reading my material. Hope is a nice thing to preserve. And in the meantime, I practice distilling my ideas down to their essence—that is what the writers' conference really taught me.

To Be Creative is, in Fact, Canadian

Margaret Atwood

Mr. Harper is wrong: There's more to the arts than a bunch of rich people at galas whining about their grants

What sort of country do we want to live in? What sort of country do we already live in? What do we like? Who are we?

At present, we are a very creative country. For decades, we've been punching above our weight on the world stage—in writing, in popular music, and in may other fields. Canada was once a cultural void on the world map, now it's a force. In addition, the arts are a large segment of our economy. The Conference Board estimates Canada's cultural sector generated $46 billion, or 3.8 per cent of Canada's GDP, in 2007. And according to Canada Council, in 2003-2004, the sector accounted for an "estimated 600,000 jobs (roughly the same as agriculture, forestry, fishing, mining, oil and gas, and utilities combined)."

But we've just been sent a signal by Prime Minister Harper that he gives not a toss for these facts. Tuesday, he told us that some group called "ordinary people" didn't care about something called "the arts." His idea of "the arts" is a bunch of rich people gathering at galas whining about their grants. Well, I can count the number of moderately rich writers who live in Canada on the fingers of one hand: I'm one of them, and I'm no Warren Buffet. I don't whine about my grants because I don't get any grants. I whine about other grants—grants for young people, that may help them to turn into me, and thus pay to the federal and provincial governments the kinds of taxes I pay, and cover off the salaries of such as Mr. Harper. In fact, less than 10 per cent of writers actually make a living by their writing, however, modest that living may be. They have other jobs. But people write, and want to write, and pack into creative writing classes, because they love this activity—not because they think they'll be millionaires.

Every single one of these people is an "ordinary person." Mr. Harper's idea of an ordinary person is that of an envious hater without a scrap of artistic talent or creativity or curiosity, and no appreciation for anything that's attractive or beautiful. My idea of an ordinary person is quite different. Human beings are creative by nature. For millenniums we have been putting our creativity into our cultures—cultures with unique languages, architectures, religious ceremonies, dances, music, furnishings, textiles, clothing, and special cuisines. "Ordinary people" pack into the cheap seats at concerts and fill theatres where operas are brought to them live. The total attendance for "the arts" in Canada in fact exceeds that for sports events. "The arts" are not a "niche interest." They are part of being human.

Moreover, "ordinary people" are participants. They form book clubs, and join classes of all kinds—painting, dancing, pottery, photography—for the sheer joy of it. They sing in choirs, church and other, and play in marching bands. Kids start garage bands and make their own videos and web art, and put their music on the Net, and draw their own graphic novels. "Ordinary people" have other outlets for their creativity as well: Knitting and quilting have made comebacks; gardening is taken very seriously; the home woodworking shop is active. Add origami, costume design, egg decorating, flower arranging, and on and on ... Canadians, it seems, like making things, and they like appreciating things that are made.

They show this appreciation by contributing. Canadians of all ages volunteer in vast numbers for local and city museums, for their art galleries and for countless cultural festivals—I think immediately of the Chinese New Year and the Caribana festival in Toronto, but there are so many others. Literary festivals have sprung up all over the country—volunteers set them up and provide the food, and "ordinary people" will drag their lawn chairs into a field—as in Nova Scotia's Read by the Sea—in order to listen to writers both local and national read and discuss their work. Mr. Harper has signalled that as far as he is concerned, those millions of hours of volunteer activity are a waster of them. He holds them in contempt.

I suggest considering the huge amount of energy we spend on creative activity, to be creative is "ordinary." It is an age-long and normal human characteristic: All children are born creative. It's the lack of appreciation of these activities that is not ordinary. Mr. Harper has demonstrated that he has no knowledge of, or respect for, the capacities and interests of "ordinary people." He's the "niche interest." Not us.

It's been suggested that Mr. Harper's disdain for the arts is not merely a result of ignorance or a tin ear—that it is "ideologically motivated." Now, I wonder what could be meant by that? Mr. Harper has said quite rightly that people understand we ought to keep within a budget. But his own contribution to that budget has been to heave the Liberal-generated surplus overboard so we have nothing left for a rainy day, and now, in addition, he wants to jeopardize those 600,000 arts jobs and those billions of dollars they generate for Canadians. What's the idea here? That arts jobs should not exist because artists are naughty and might not vote for Mr. Harper? That Canadians ought not to make money from the wicked arts, but only from virtuous oil? That artists don't all live in one constituency, so who cares? Or is it that the majority of those arts jobs are located in Ontario and Quebec, and Mr. Harper is peeved at those provinces, and wants to increase his ongoing gutting of Ontario–$20 billion a year of Ontario taxpayers' money going out, a dribble grudgingly allowed back in—and spank Quebec for being so disobedient as to not appreciate his magnificence? He likes punishing, so maybe the arts-squashing is part of that: Whack the Heartland.

Or is it even worse? Every budding dictatorship begins by muzzling the artists, because they're a mouthy lot and they don't line up and salute very easily. Of course, you can always get some tame artists to design the uniforms and flags and the documentary about you, and so forth—the only kind of art you might need—but individual voices must be silenced, because there shall be only One Voice: Our Master's Voice. Maybe that's why Mr. Harper began by shutting down funding for our artists abroad. He didn't like the competition for media space.

The Conservative caucus has already learned that lesson. Rumour has it that Mr. Harper's idea of what sort of art you should hang on your wall was signalled by his removal of all pictures of previous Conservative prime ministers from their lobby room—including John A. and Dief the Chief—and their replacement by pictures of none other than Mr. Harper himself. History, it seems, is to begin with him. In communist countries, this used to be called the Cult of Personality. Mr. Harper is a guy who—rumour has it, again—tried to disband the student union in high school and then tried the same thing in college. Destiny is calling him, the way it called Qin Shi Huang, the Chinese emperor who burnt all records of the rulers before himself. It's an impulse that's been repeated many times since, the list is very long. "Tear it down and level it flat" is the common motto. Then build a big statue of yourself. Now that would be Art!

Adapted from the 2008 Hurtig Lecture, delivered in Edmonton on October 1. Reprinted from The Globe and Mail *and* The Writers' Union of Canada Newsletter *with permission from the author.*

WRITE

Eric Solomon

[*Write*, implies John Lee. Write positively about a philosophy of life and the world we live in. Uplift! But I am not Dr. Feelgood, cheerily flourishing in this universe of Dr. Strangeloves. Shall I imitate W.H. Auden who underestimated the longevity of his "low, dishonest decade" of the 1930s, which now is even lower and more dishonest? Shall I resonate with boyish laughter at being asked to write anything as I start my ninth decade? Deal with joyous memories when I can't really recall who John Lee is? Praise old friends when I have gone to five memorial services in two weeks? Recall my 401 K? Praise my wife, children, grandchildren, while sustaining my basic anxious, paranoid symptoms? Plus deal with odd lower back pain? And my writing has always been sardonic, negative, ironic, mordant. What? How? Why?]

I do have a comparatively recent positive formula for coping with threatening universal—simplistic, yes. Possible, probably not. And like all philosophies, as the narrative voice of *The Great Gatsby* elucidates, my uplifting words are easy to write, but most probably impossible to follow. Still, here is an oldster's try. Whatever.

When I turned sixty-seven, I paused for a rare moment of reflection. I assumed that I would live to be one hundred—not illogical since my father lasted ninety years, my mother ninety-seven, and I can only work with round numbers. Thus, I had lived two-thirds of my span, and the years had been largely positive: much love from family, many friends, good health, professional and financial success, (Ha!) a plethora of books and articles produced, being at once a progressive rebel and a cool administrator ... Sure, there were the disasters, losses, betrayals, times of despair and fear, but this span had earned an A-/B+. Still, what logic could ask for thirty-three more good years? Betrayals loomed. My body would turn the pulled muscles and lower back twinges into serious calamities. My short-term memory, attention span, night vision ... fuzziness would prevail. And the cruellest betrayals, the deaths of loved ones, friends, admired authors, art forms, political heroes ... many if not all sources of pleasure and emotional losses would join mental and physical disasters. How to think or write positively?

I am one who has tried to teach people to write; I believe in the topic sentence and forceful thesis statement. Here goes. For the last period of this game of life, I would live by the bromidic cliché "one day at a time." More important than the pleasure of small twenty-four hour victories, I would bank, in calming ways, these survivals. And no more varieties of road rage against evil drivers, politicians, bankers ... No more metaphorical horn honking or giving the finger—not out of fear the other driver may have a gun, but out of gratitude that I still can drive, or walk, or 'live.' Thus, "one day at a time," and be kind. As all baseball fans should know, extra innings are fascinating, suspenseful, and the game *must* end. Still, as a great American poet, Woody Guthrie, put it, "Take it easy. But take it."

3

When the Money Loves Us

John B. Lee

Imagine a childless widow in the final stages of terminal cancer. Imagine that she is endowed with a considerable estate amounting in value to over a half a million dollars. Imagine that she is the loving aunt of two devoted children of her eldest sister. Imagine that she has willed her entire holdings to this niece and nephew, with codicils leaving small sums to each of the children of these two beloved individuals. Imagine a close relationship where this childless aunt is invited to participate in every family get together. Every Easter, every Thanksgiving, every Christmas, every birthday, anniversary, graduation, she is included, welcomed, and joyfully involved.

Imagine then a vacation in Mexico, prior to the onset of ill health. Imagine this aunt joining this niece, this nephew, their spouses, and their respective children on the beach in celebration of bonds forged over nearly fifty years of consanguinity and fellowship. Imagine this as being the last and lasting impression of a final time together. Imagine that she has brought with her the commonplace book of her mother wherein that ancestor to them all has kept a written record of the daily lives of herself and her children. "You'll get this when I pass away," she says.

Imagine that when she returns from this vacation she begins to feel poorly and after seeking doctor's council she discovers that she is very ill and dying. When she speaks with her niece on the phone, she says, "I'm very ill. I don't want visitors. I don't want you to phone me any more because I don't feel well enough to talk on the phone. I'll continue to keep you informed through your brother, and I'll see him often because he knows I'm not well, and he can visit me with ease since we live in the same city. Please honour my wishes, and don't be hurt."

Imagine the nephew visiting the ailing aunt almost every day. Imagine a conversation in which the aunt informs him, "I've decided to give my neighbour Power of Attorney. It's more convenient for him. He's right next door and he's promised to provide me with everything I need. Otherwise, nothing has changed."

Imagine a month passing. Imagine the aunt becoming so ill she can no longer have visitors. Imagine that she is so ill the doctor is making house calls. Imagine the day she dies, the nephew sits alone at her bedside holding her hand as he feels her slip away. When he comes from the dying room and enters the kitchen, he discovers the neighbour there with a stranger having a very animated conversation. The neighbour, it seems, has called this stranger to the house. The nephew thinks it must be the coroner. He wipes his eyes and composes himself to say hello.

Imagine the day of the funeral. The nephew arrives to discover that the funeral director is confused about the protocol for the day. The brother-in-law has prepared a eulogy. "You will speak at my funeral some day," the aunt has told the niece's husband who has been a speaker at the funeral of many loved ones. The funeral director says, "It doesn't seem that you are involved at all. I'll have to ask permission for your brother-in-law to speak. It seems the neighbour of the deceased is in charge of every detail." This fact comes as a shock to the nephew. Feathers are smoothed and an opportunity to 'say a few words' has been accommodated by the neighbour.

The lawyer of the aunt enters the funeral home. The nephew recognizes her as the same person he saw in the kitchen talking in an animated way with the neighbour on the day of his aunt's passing. Not suspicious by nature, he makes nothing of this at this point.

Following the service the nephew asks the lawyer about the reading of the will and the lawyer says, "Oh, you're not involved in *that*. That's for those who are in the will."

"May I see a copy of the will?"

For whatever reason the lawyer produces a copy of the will and delivers it to the nephew who informs his sister, "We have been disowned."

The nephew and the niece are satisfied that this must be the desire of their aunt. All they want at this point is a jar of chili sauce made by their aunt and the commonplace book written in the hand of their grandmother. A few days after the funeral the nephew phones the neighbour and requests the chili sauce and the book and he is told by the neighbour, "Of course, but let me figure out what they're worth and I'll give you a price."

At this point the nephew finally comes to a boil and replies, "Fuck you! I'll see you in court."

The nephew discovers that the final will and testament of his beloved aunt leaves everything to the neighbour. This same neighbour who when she knew the aunt was about to die left her side and phoned the lawyer to come over to the house. This was the exchange witnessed by the nephew only moments after departing from the bedside of his aunt at whose side he had stayed while she passed. This same neighbour, a self-confessed poor person had only months before purchased a brand new car, renovated the house and added a paved driveway and garage to their property. This same neighbour who had taken the ailing woman out of her sickbed when she was considered too ill to have visitors and when even the doctor was making house calls because of her weakness, had taken her to the lawyer to draft a new will leaving everything she owned to the neighbour according to a handwritten document composed in the hand of the neighbour.

Imagine this neighbour as she consigns to the fire the commonplace book of the family disinherited by her hand. Imagine the stories burning, the recipes in flame, the ashes of a childhood gone up in smoke. Imagine the ten mason jars of chili sauce tossed into the nuisance ground. Imagine how the money loves her then.

There's Something About Hospital Corridors

John Wing

There's something about hospital corridors. Yes, they're clean and smell of that cleanliness, not oily and smelling of piss and vomit like an urban alley. But an alley has life in it. It smells of life that's passed through. A hospital corridor has death in it. Antiseptic, white-sheeted death. Funny, since I was born in this hospital. My father walked my mother in and waved goodbye, then went and smoked until they came and told him he had a son. I walked along the deserted hall, remembering life and feeling death.

I had flown almost three thousand miles to this corridor, and at the end of it, now getting closer, was my father. He had been here thirty-one days. A visit to the doctor had finally been scheduled, most probably months after he had noticed something wrong with his foot, and the doctor tested it even though he knew damn well what it was. Gangrene. My father had undoubtedly known too, before he went in. He was not a stupid man, just a stubborn and a timid one. The doctor had offered him a simple choice. Don't treat it, go home and die. Or have the foot amputated. My father, who had spent a grand total of two nights in a hospital in his 78 years (and that included the night he was born), elected to have the foot cut off.

He had lived his life without much caring for what we modernists would call health. Ate what he wanted, drank a fair amount (Some would say a lot), smoked, never exercised other than golf, which he stopped playing almost twenty years before, didn't walk, run, or work out. He lived so he would die quickly. Talking one minute, then clutching and then dead. He spoke often with envy of those who had gone that way. He feared death more than anyone I had ever known, and tried to make certain his would be swift and relatively painless. But he lost the bet.

I had been on the road and lived on the other side of the continent, so I got daily phone and e-mail briefings from my sister, who had suspended her plans for the spring and gone to be with my parents, hoping to take some of the strain off my mother. I was attempting to prepare myself that he might die on the table, but he got through it, it was an act, I knew, of enormous courage for him. And he was not by nature a courageous man. He was so afraid of flying that he had never come to visit me in the 20 years I had lived on the other coast. He simply would not do anything he found scary. But he did this. I was proud of him. When I called to tell him I was coming, I asked if there was anything I could bring him. He said, Oh, you know what I need. I realized he said it that way because my mother and my sister had been in the room. But I did know what he wanted. Smokes. And now, walking down the hall, three hours from my plane landing, tired and a bit jet-lagged, I had in my pocket a pack of special cigarettes. English Ovals. Long, non-filtered, and delicious. It had been a few years since I'd had a cigarette, but I knew how good these were, and I'd purchased them especially for Dad.

I come from a family of smokers. My parents and both sets of grandparents were smokers. In the sixties, when the surgeon general's report finally proved what everyone with a brain had already known, it was too late for my mother's father, who succumbed to lung cancer at age 68. My mother and her sister had promptly quit, and though my mother had a hard time of it, eventually she gave it up for good. My father's parents smoked all through their lives. His mother died at 82, and his father at 92.

In fact, the last time I visited my grandfather in the nursing home sixteen years before this, he'd asked me to bring him smokes. (He also asked me to help him break out). My father attempted to quit smoking in the late sixties. He had gone eight days without a cigarette. On the eighth day, he had eaten nine small meals at a diner near his office. The ninth day he want back smoking, and never left again. Despite doctor's dire warnings, he continued to smoke roughly two packs of non-filtered Camels a day. He was the last holdout in the family now. And he had lived to see smoking banned everywhere, except his house. So he rarely left home.

But today was his thirty-first day without a cigarette. My mother and sister were effusive in their praise about it, even as he continued to insist that he would be starting again as soon as he got home. But that was still at least six weeks away, if not more. He had physiotherapy and lots of counselling left to do, plus a prosthesis to be fitted and made. My mother felt it would be easy for him to stay off cigarettes after he'd gone three months. I wondered if she'd forgive me for what I was about to do.

Many years before, I'd made a decision regarding my Dad. I wanted to be his friend, as well as his son. Perhaps, somewhere in the crazy competitiveness that existed in our family, mostly because of him, I wanted to be the best loved, or best liked child. It didn't matter now. I had decided not to bother him about his failings. To nag him genially, as mother did, and which he despised, or to confront him directly about what a lazy stupid bastard he was, as my younger brother did, I don't think he loved them any less for their obvious concern, but he was always a man who prized, above all things, minding your own business. And, when you got right down to it, how much he smoked or drank, how much he exercised, or not, was simply not my business. It was his. So be it.

It relieved our relationship of a lot of stress, because as I came to adulthood and beyond, he practiced what he had always preached with me. If I asked for advice, he would freely give it, but mostly, we minded our own affairs. He still felt compelled to criticize me at times, occasionally in a loud voice that would frighten anyone who didn't know him, but I developed ways to deflect and gently remind him of our unspoken pact. I grew a goatee in my early forties and he thought it looked ridiculous. The third or fourth time he started in on me about it, I waited until he'd finished, and then said, My wife likes it. Which had an amazing effect. He shut up and never mentioned it again. Later in that same visit, I made some sort of mistake at the dinner table and he laid into me about it. Oddly, I have no recollection of what it was, but he started off in his voice of doom. My mother looked down into her soup and waited for it to end, but I didn't let him go, keeping my eyes on his, staying calm. Then, as he wound up, I reached into my pocket, extracted my wallet, pulled out my passport, opened it to the picture page, and handed it across the table to him. What the hell is this? he asked, looking at it. Note my age, I replied quietly, I was forty-three at the time, and I think he got the message. You can't talk to me like that anymore.

But still, my plan had worked. We were friends. I don't know if he knew how much I loved him, but aside from my wife and children, he was the most important relationship of my life. And here I was, trying again to be his friend. To win his approval. To do the thing he wanted me to do. I got off the elevator at the long-term care floor and turned toward his room, which was at the end of the hall.

As I had hoped, the nurse on duty at the main desk didn't even look up when I passed. I walked past rooms, trying not to look in but getting fleeting glances of despair in each one. Even asleep, people in hospitals look pathetic. I arrived at his room and went in. It was a two patient suite, with a curtain between the beds. Dad was on the far side, the window side. The man in the first bed nodded to me and, hearing the footsteps, my father called, Who is it? His voice was strong, as usual. Even as his living choices had ravaged his face and body, that voice remained just as it was when I was small. It made our phone call relationship perfect because he never seemed to age there. The man in the other bed said, I think it's your son.

I came around the curtain and there he was. Drawn and certainly thinner, minus a foot, and in a completely alien place for both of us, but he was alive and his face lit up when he saw me. Jake! He called, with genuine pleasure. Thanks for coming to see me.

I took off my coat and sat down by his bed, moving the walker. We held hands for a while and talked about my business and of what was going on with my wife and children, the two things he always asked about first in our phone conversations. I tried to keep a reasonably happy look on my face, but it was chilling to see him here. He was weak, and all his frailties were on full display. Things I'd only had the barest glimpses of throughout my life. Seeing him in bed was almost funny. When we were children, he used to go upstairs to watch television in his bedroom, and if there was something I wanted to watch that wasn't being viewed downstairs, I would sometimes sneak up there and watch while he was asleep. A couple of times he was awake when I crept in. He would be lying on his bed, naked, reading a paperback. When I opened the door, he would place the paperback over his genitals, covering himself and bookmarking at the same time. If I got in safely without waking him, he would be asleep with the book spread across his groin. It was an image that one keeps.

I didn't mention the image. There were others to occupy me, anyway. His left foot, or lack of it, was heavily bandaged and looked like a club. He was wearing sweat pants, which looked odd on him. On the floor was a single running shoe. Again, odd, since he never wore those either. The walker was in one corner and a folded up wheelchair was in the other. While we were talking, the night nurse came in. She smiled at us. How are you feeling tonight, Mr. Wing? she asked. He gave her a look of unmitigated scorn, and replied, I'm in the hospital. She laughed, for which I was grateful. She did her checking

Reading hands *photo by Marty Gervais (M.G.)*

Detroit, Woodward Avenue *(M.G.)*

Sweeping the barn *(M.G.)*

Going to work *(M.G.)*

Former Canadian Motor Lamp

photo by Mike Beauchamps (M.B.)

Elmwood Diner *(M.G.)*

Detroit mural *(M.G.)*

Windsor night scene *(M.G.)*

Abandoned parking lot for Tiger Stadium, Detroit *(M.G.)*

Pawnbroker shops on Michigan Avenue, Detroit
photo by Sarah St. Pierre (S.S.P.)

Detroit *(S.S.P.)*

Apartment complex, Detroit *(S.S.P.)*

and left. Then he turned and finally asked, Did you bring the smokes? I nodded and mentioned how great it was that he'd gone thirty-one days and maybe he should try to go a little longer. He didn't smile. He said he'd been dreaming about it, couldn't stop the wanting. It was all he thought about. I said it does get better, you know. No, I don't fucking know, he replied. It's never gotten better with me. I made one final attempt and his face got very hard. His little, I-can't-believe-I-have-to-listen-to-this-shit-in-my-own-house face. I sighed and brought the cigarette package from my pocket. His eyes gleamed. I said maybe we should wait until tomorrow, since it is very cold outside. He shook his head and indicated his tiny closet, which held a heavy jacket. I got it out and he sat up, swinging his legs over. Bring me the walker, he said. He showed me how to place it, and as he struggled to get off the bed, I got the wheelchair out and opened it up. It was something I'd never done before, but luckily it was simple. We manoeuvred him into it and I got the coat on him, and put the scarf around his neck. I found a thick blanket and wrapped his legs and then put on the running shoe.

I left him sitting there for a moment, and went to check the hallway. It was empty. When I returned, he said What the hell were you looking for? I explained that I didn't want the nurse to catch us going out. He looked surprised. She can't stop us, he said, and I realized he was right.

I pushed him out and down the hall. We passed the nurses' station and no one was there. To the elevator and down and then another long deserted hall. We came to the door and I stopped and put my baseball cap on his head. He asked why I was doing that and I told him that, in the cold, you lose most of your body heat through the top of your head. Bullshit, he replied, but he left it on. We went out and I opened the pack and gave him one. Then I got out matches and lit it, as he had taught me. Hold the end of the match between your first and second fingers. Press it against the book with your thumb, and drag it so when it lights, it's protected by the cup of your hand. He drew greedily and exhaled the first lungful he'd had in over a month with an audible sigh of pleasure. I was putting the pack back in my pocket when he said, Will you join me? Why the hell not. I lit one and we smoked. It was a really frigid March night. The snow was packed hard, ice on the top, as if it wasn't ever going to go away this year. Around the corner was the high school I had attended. Fifty feet in front of us was where my mother had stopped, coming in to deliver me, and sat on the curb to wait for a contraction to pass. My father had stood there that night, feeling helpless, as I felt now.

The Old Man's Hour

John B. Lee

at the end
my father felt
mostly the fear of falling to
the unforgiving floor
and so we walked together
his hand
fogging my wrist
like a greying darkness
I could reach through
to find the weight of bone
the blue moment
the almost reified shadow
of his soul
and in that sadness
in that coming on
of the strength of sorrow
in the gown-gap
of his johnny shirt
and at what is now
become an old man's hour
let us call it
the ghost of woe
of each footstep's lamentation
in those slipper sounds
of a weak-hearted moving
what the oat pail wants
banged empty
what the water drum

wishes with the going still
of its shining meniscus
dulled by spill
in a dirt-dead field
where the stone boat
dragged all the dry thirst
of a long-forgotten day
where I'm once again weathered in sheep

and now, with father four years gone
his brother
sits tethered to a chair
his forehead port-stained
by knock-out
in a hospital hall
his wrist
cracked in a cast

I'm left grieving the oak
in the otherwise empty clearing
that storm-trimmed
monumental wind-loss
that comes in the night
when we are not there
but dreaming

The Middle of the End

Andrew Johnson

Living an hour up the road, I received the later-than-I-like-to-talk phone call. It was S., my sister-in-law. In the eight years since I had moved away from Chatham, S. had never called. We just didn't have that kind of relationship.

Dad's in intensive care at St. Joe's.

She'd always called him *Dad.* I'd always liked that.

Your brother and Dad didn't want to tell you. You know what they're like. Dad took Mom's van out to the farm and ran it into one of those ditches out there. They had to go in to stop the bleeding. You'd better come home.

I asked if anyone had told Mom. She said *No.*

My parents were together but my mother was across the country in Calgary to be with my sister who had had her own surgery. She had breast cancer. When I told my mother about what had happened and the shape my father was in, she just listened.

The only thing she said was, *What can I do?*

Even if every detail and assumption wasn't exactly right, she knew what had happened. Without someone to keep track of things my father would start early, fall asleep in the chair, and start over again. At some point he would long to see his little piece of ground, his 25 acres out on the 10th Concession of Dover Township. After he'd lost his license they'd sold his pickup, so my mother's van would have to do.

She told him straight out before she left not to even think about touching that van, but there he'd go out the Bear Line and cut up to the Winter Line on some route that would take him by Armand Boudreau's, Joe Pinsonneault's, Don Cadotte's. Because he was a bit pissed he wouldn't turn into anyone's driveway, but he'd be comforted to know their trucks were there, that his old friends were still kicking. Then he'd get to the farm, the place he'd sold a few years back when he couldn't get out there because they had taken his license. They took his license away because his eyes were failing as fast as his hearing and his left knee. He'd really just needed to see the place. To know that it was still there, that he could get there and that he had worked *that* land.

Then what happened? Did he crank his neck around to glance back at the farm, squinting to see if they had cut down any of the trees we'd planted soon after he'd bought the place? Then did he turn the wheel just enough to send him into the deep ditch first cut better than 100 years before to make marsh arable land. He'd tell me that the fact that it was once marsh was the thing that made the land so rich, that made the corn grow so fast you could hear it.

I didn't get any clear answers. No one seemed able to say. What I did know was that with no seatbelt on, the steering wheel crushed his already swollen and tender insides.

No answers came from my father. They kept him sedated, pain-free. When he drifted into near-consciousness he took no part in the present. Instead, he mumbled about *skating the river*, perhaps the nearby Sydenham when he was a boy. More unsettling was when he seemed to be back in England, back in a war he rarely spoke about in his lucid moments. Agitated, he needed to *get back*, but there was *no light, not one light. Blackout, God damned black-*

out. I said, *Dad, where are you?* Quiet now, he seemed only able to stumble through his darkness. As he shook and cried and hallucinated I sat by his bed in intensive care watching the nurses come and go, watching the Thames River move slow.

I am not sure how I got out there, but I went to the OPP station to see my mother's smashed van. It was too far for me to walk, so it must have been my brother or my cousin P. An officer let me in so I could retrieve the ownership and insurance papers. I needed them so I could send the thing off to see if anyone could put it back together. I knew my mother would be heartbroken *and* mad as hell if it were her standing in front of the van. I just marvelled at the impact. The front was totally crumpled and thick with Dover clay.

The only person I can remember being at the station was the officer. He backed up his moralizing discourse with words that sounded like facts. *I understand that the driver's license was not renewed due to poor eyesight* and *I understand that a DUI charge was contemplated by the officer on the scene*. What could I say but *yes sir*. Incontestable. Predictable. Unfortunate. What more could I say? This was not who I wanted to talk to.

I wanted to say, *come talk to me when your world closes in, when your eyes fail, when gout bites your knees, when you can't hear the news on the television, when they yank out your gall bladder and tell you what you can never eat again. Tell me if you want to accept it, or if you will fight even if you know you will lose*. Instead I kept my mouth shut and made the arrangements to have the van sent to the shop.

Once my father's eyes were open and the nurses made

him sit up in bed and try to eat., I knew that it was time for me to go. Before I left we didn't talk about what happened or why.

4

HARD TIMES—GETTING FIRED

Robert Sward

MONEY, INSPIRATION, AND THE MUSE

In a capitalist country, money is oxygen. As someone plagued by asthma, I find an inverse relationship between the amount of money I have in the bank and the need for inhalers. When I'm in debt, I struggle for breath. When I'm free of debt, I breathe easy. Money is oxygen. Question: what is the relationship between money and the muse? For myself, it's closer than you think.

Still, speaking as a writer, I find the only thing better than being employed is being unemployed. Santa Cruz Operation paid well and offered any number of benefits to departing employees. I was virtually given a Macintosh computer with that, plus unemployment benefits, I set to work on *Four Incantations: New and Selected Poems* which was later published by Coffee House Press.

"Ah, that reminds me of a joke," said the programmer at my 'farewell party.'" A man goes to a doctor and the doc says, "You have a book in you and I'm afraid it's going to have to come out."

As William Stafford once observed, "Every emergency is also an opportunity."

The end of every story is the beginning of another. That may also be a cliché, but it's true.

1.

PERSONAL STRESS ASSESSMENT

(Found Poem)

Make a list of all the life events that apply to you …
then add them up with the points assigned.

To be married and moderately unhappy
is less stressful than to be unmarried
and male and over 30.
To be happily married counts for 0 points.
If your spouse dies that counts for 100 points.
63 for going to jail. 73 for divorce.
Divorce is more stressful than imprisonment.
Getting married is 3 points more stressful
than being fired. Marital reconciliation (45 points)
and retirement (also 45 points)
are only half as stressful as
the death of your spouse.
Minor violations of the law: 11 points.
Trouble with the boss: 23. Christmas: 12. But
sexual difficulties are less stressful
than pregnancy (40 points versus 39).
A mortgage over $10,000 is worse
than a son (or daughter) leaving home.
Trouble with your in-laws is as stressful
as "outstanding personal achievement"
which is only slightly more stressful
than if "wife begins or stops work."

Are you very happy and well-adjusted? 0 points.
Very angry, depressed or frustrated? 20 points.

Conclusion: With 25 points or more, "you probably will feel better if you reduce your stress."

2.

Good News from the Other World

Palm Springs, CA

"Dad, you're lookin' good," I say,
"like the fountain of youth."

His hands on my feet, grimacing, weary,
mercurial, wing-footed
eighty-year-old doctor.

Wears a denim shirt, bola tie,
turquoise and silver tip,
tanned, tennis-playing, macho…

"Making more money now,
more than in Skokie.
But you need arch supports," he says,
encasing my feet in plaster.

Damaged feet. Feet out of alignment.
Four-times married, forty-year-old feet.

"Well, good news from the other world," he says.

"Really?"

"The void is nothing but people's breath."

"So something survives?" I say,

"Feet survive. Feet and breath survive," he says,
"peoples' feet and peoples' breath."

"That *is* good news," I say.

"Don't mock me," he says.
"Do you know you still 'toe in'?
That your head 'pitches forward'?
You're past the halfway mark, son.
God is not altruistic, you know,
He doesn't make exceptions.
Of course things are dark and light at once."

Huh? Who *is* he? Whoever was my father?

Bloodied in some Russian pogrom.
Nixon-lover on the North Side of Chicago.
Blue denim, bola tie Republican.

Rosicrucian cowboy in the Promised Land.

3.

HALF A LIFE'S HISTORY

(Excerpted from *The Jurassic Shales*)

Scenario: *An amnesiac wakes one morning in London, England, in bed with two women. In the process of recovering his memory, he goes back in time 160 million years to the Jurassic geological period to find his true original parents, the first of the flying dinosaurs. The narrator is himself a flying dinosaur, and* The Jurassic Shales *ends with his being united with his father and mother.*

Here I am writing to you
half a life's history
"A horse which throws the dreamer to the ground."
I am homesick and America has had a nervous
breakdown.
I am taking shaman lessons and studying Karate.
My greatest complaint (you've offered to help) is
amnesia.
Do you believe in transmigration of the soul? Yes, I do too.
But what if it can happen not only when one dies, but
several times in an afternoon?
And I'm sure it's not properly amnesia I am speaking of.
I go out of my body, I come back in.
I say amnesia because sometimes when this happens
I forget just who I am.
I've been doing this, I believe, with some regularity
for a quarter of a million years. I'm doing it more
and more frequently now because I'm unhappy.

Even the light depresses me. That is, the light
on Oxford Street, 6 PM on a Sunday. The light
in Bloom's. The light in Wimpy's. I haven't seen
light like this since the Middle Ages of the Animals.

We drink, we smoke, we go to parties. Friday night
we went to the dullest party in 3,000 years
in Bayswater off the Moscow Road.
I thought the whole time of algae, worms,
primitive brachiopods, mollusks, crustaceans,
I thought of my mother and those birds with the hollow
bones.
I am in the library at Swiss Cottage
eating chocolates in the children's room
What am I reading? Probably I have gone mad.
I am reading up on the eohippus, the first true
archaic horse.
I identify. Those horses were no larger than dogs.
I'm a dog and interested in horses
that were once my own size.
Why? I don't know why. Yes, I do. It's because
I feel I was once (also) a woolly rhinoceros.
That I am at this moment a woolly rhinoceros.
Anyway, I am no longer incapacitated by my erotic
fantasies.
I am devoting my whole attention to insects, geology,
etc.
Each morning I have friends come in to read me my
biography and my passport.
Then I know who I am. Then I can pay attention
to what needs to be done.

Who are these people anyway? They think they speak English,
    but I don't understand a word they say.
My only reason for coming was to learn Karate with Kanazawa,
    who has left for Germany.
Oh, I've just gone out of my body and now I'm back.
What is happening in America where, I am convinced,
    in my previous existence, I was a Confederate
    soldier killed in action, 186-?
Well, it doesn't matter. I'll find out soon enough and probably
    know anyway if I'd only think about it.

4.

ON MY WAY TO THE KOREAN WAR...

For President Dwight Eisenhower

On my way to the Korean War,
I never got there.
One summer afternoon in 1952,
I stood instead in the bow
of the Attack Transport *Menard*,
with an invading force
of 2,000 battle-ready Marines,
watching the sun go down.
Whales and porpoises,
flying fish and things jumping
out of the water.
Phosphoresence—

Honolulu behind us,
Inchon, Korea, and the war ahead.

Crew cut, 18-year-old librarian,
Yeoman 3rd Class, editor
of the ship's newspaper,
I wrote critically if unoriginally
of our Commander-in-Chief,
Mr. President,
and how perplexing it was that he
would launch a nuclear-powered submarine
while invoking the Lord,
Crocodile Earth shaker,
Shiva J. Thunderclap,
choosing the occasion to sing
the now famous *Song of the Armaments*,
the one with the line "weapons for peace":

> O weapons for peace,
> O weapons for peace,
> awh want, awh want
> more weapons for peace!

At sundown, a half dozen sailors
converged on the bow of the ship
where, composed and silent,
we'd maintain our vigil
until the sun had set.

Careful to avoid being conspicuous,
no flapping or flailing of the arms,

no running, horizontal take-offs,
one man, then another, stepped out into space,
headed across the water,
moving along as if on threads.
After a while, I did the same:
left my body just as they left theirs.

In-breathe, out-breathe, and leave,
in-breathe, out-breathe, and leave.
Leave your body, leave your body,
leave your body, leave your body,

we sang as we went out
to where the light went,
and whatever held us to that ship
and its 2,000 battle-ready troops, let go.
So it was, dear friends, I learned to fly.
And so in time must you
and so will the warships,
and the earth itself,
and the sky,
for as the prophet says, the day cometh
when there will be no earth left to leave.

O me, O my,
O me, O my,
goodbye earth, goodbye sky.
Goodbye, goodbye.

5.

What Was God Thinking?

1. *At the Hospital*

Father:
"I don't understand. What was God thinking,
what was He thinking?"

Mother:
"What's to understand?
I'm dead.
We weren't made to last.
What's to understand?
Ach, he doesn't hear me."

"God forgive me.
A good woman. At least may she rest in peace."

"Rest in peace? I'm dead for god sake.
What good will rest do?
You rest in peace. And something
else, my friend, no viewing,
no 'open casket.' They want to look at me, let them
go look at someone else. Later,
if they want to visit, fine.
They know the address.
But no flowers. Tell them. No flowers.
Flowers die.
Stones they should bring, not flowers.
And as for afterlife, tell them, there is no 'afterlife.'
Look at him. He doesn't hear a word I'm saying."

2. *The End of the World*

"He stripped your mother, son,
        stripped the soul from her body.
You think a human life is not a world?
So then mourn,
        mourn for the end of the world.
And cover the mirrors.
Oi, look at you:
        Take off those shoes.
This is not a time for leather.
Here, let me tear that shirt for you.
Why? Because your mother's dead. God did her in;
her death should cost you something too.
That's right and put ashes on your head.
You're sitting *shiva* now.
        It's the law. You're a Jew.
Read the small print.
Seven days you cannot leave the house.
No radio, no TV, no looking at magazines,
        no books.
You'll see what death is like.
She's gone, so mourn, damn you, mourn!"

6.

Anniversary of Her Death

At the Rosicrucian Altar

Sweeps away incense and candles,
        liquid-filled crystal flask…
"Forget prayer, forget everything I ever said."
Bolts the door, pours himself a drink.

Said about what, dad?

"What? Prayer. *Everything*. Forget it!
God doesn't need your prayer.
Now put on your shoes and get out of here."

But dad, this stuff is just beginning
to make sense.

"Nonsense," he says.

What about the unseen?

"Goddammit, if it isn't seen,
        it isn't there.
She's dead. Your mother's dead.

What are you, stupid?"
Reaches for matches. Lights a cigarette.

But what about… soul?

"Soul? You know better than that.
There is no soul."

"There is no other side. You want to know
what's on the other side? Nothing.
That's what's on the other side.
Ach, you're looking for meaning.
        Meaning's on backorder.
The sun and the moon and the stars,
        they're all on backorder.
Nothing's there. Nothing ever existed.
        She's dead. Don't you get it? The world is just
        a word.
Talmud says.
        Earth is a flaming word.
That's it. That's it. End of story."

DARKNESS IS A CANDLE TOO

7.

AFTER THE BYPASS

Palm Springs, CA

1. *In The Hospital*

"Don't trust the world, son. It's filled
with holes. The best thing is to love..."

Love what, dad?

"Emptiness. I've been meaning to tell you:
There's a giant scroll suspended below the world
and it says this world
is made from letters and numbers
and every number is infinite.
Anyway, I'm invisible, son."

Dad, I can see you.

"You have two fathers,
one you can see,
one who looks like me;
and one you can't,
the father you'll never see.
The invisible *is* invisible,
but I need to make a living.
I'm a doctor, *nu?* What good is a doctor
if you can't see him?

Don't look at me like that. I'm still a Jew,
but some days all I see is Roses and Crosses.
Did you know the male body has nine holes in it?
Seven of those holes are in the head. So there you have it.
The world is a leaky boat, son."

2. *Checking Out*

Rosy cheeked father in a wheel chair.
He pulls out a toothpick. Makes little sucking noises
with his teeth. "Hospital food. Not as bad as they say."

Lights a cigarette.

"She's against it."

Who?

"Who do you think? She's against
the invisible."

Throws away the toothpick.

"I've fallen into a place where everything is music.
You know, if people could take a pill
and become invisible
there would be nobody in sight. It's true. The world
        is made of love,
of our love for emptiness.
Ach, what the hell! Visible, invisible,
        It's all the same.

Still, the world you go round thinking you can see
is filled with holes, and for every hole
        in this world
        there's a hole in the other. If you look,
you can see through the cracks.
I have a treasure now, it's true,
        but no body.
And you, you *meshugge*, you have a body,
but no treasure.
You should take the year off. Spend some time
at the Invisible College."

3. *Course of Study*

Lesson #1

"Stars ejaculate. That's how the world
        came into being.
From sperm. The Sperm of the Stars."

Lesson #2

"There is no place empty of God.

"Darkness is a candle, too.

"So open the window in your chest.
Let the invisible fly in and out."

Lesson #3

"The invisible is more existent than all the visible things.
Talmud says.
Still, when you leave your body there's not much to
stand on.
And there's a crack in the cosmic egg.
Truth is, this world is just one side of the nothing
that's on the other side."

Lesson #4

"Now I'll tell you about death.
Life has an eye to see, says Talmud,
                                        but what do you think Death has?
Death is made of eyes,
                                        made of eyes, dressed in eyes.
And when she comes, she comes with a knife
          in her hands.
And you go through the wall and it's a flaming word.
Death is what happens when all you have left
          is the life that was there all along.
But remember: you're still gonna need money
          when you die."

Lament of a Craftsman

Sheila Tucker

There was a time when 60 wasn't old.
"Experience," "Maturity" were king.
Apprentices would ask me everything.
I showed them how to weld and cast a mold
Or beat wrought iron til it bent and rolled
In furnace heat. (You'd hear a heavy "ding"
And sparks from red-hot metal sound a ring.)
To trainees' eyes, I was the boss, the bold
And gifted guy that knew the shapes that sold.
Cast-iron Gods, wrought-iron gates and bring.
I never thought the company would sling
Me out the door and simply leave me cold.
They chose to keep two trainees. Ain't that swell?
A third my age—their pay's a third as well.

LABOUR

Don Gutteridge

for my father, putting a fieldstone front on our house

My father once borrowed
a stoneboat to haul
fieldstones (too rooted
to be purged by our fore-
bears) all the way to the
house he'd built for us block
by cinder block: "It needs
a little somethng to set it off,"
he grinned. I see him still:
    a bronzed bareback
    Centurion with sledge-
    heavy hands cracking
    open rocks as hoary
    as dinosaur eggs, then
    rearing back, wordless,
    to savour the prismed
    rivulets and pied hues
    his body-blow exposed,
    now tucking a single
    shard into its necessary
    niche with an eye as sure
    as Michelangelo's: Dad's
    mosaic: a brute beauty
    hammered out by a
    pure labour.

Seat Belt # 25

Jennifer McMullan

My life is a series of bar codes in this recession. Black isn't black. Black is PV721DVAB. Grey is PV731D5AB. After a while you forget that colours have names. Excitement becomes things you never thought could make you happy. A piece of paper that says "no parts required." A screen that declares you're at broadcast. A high screeching buzz like fingernails on a chalkboard becomes the sound you long to hear.

Each day starts and ends the same, with a seatbelt in my hand.

Seatbelts are never vibrant colours. You're trapped in a world of black, light grey, dark grey, and beige. Some days I'm living in a 1950s television set. Like most inanimate objects, you don't value it until it makes you look right at it.

The first time a seatbelt demanded my attention was when it saved my life. The car in front swerved. This resulted in my dad slamming on the brakes, my brother smashing his nose, and at two-years-old the seatbelt leaving a welt across my neck. If it hadn't been for that seatbelt the story could have ended very differently.

To think of the times I disregarded it as if it was nothing. The times I was angry at wearing it for messing up my outfit. The times I handled it roughly as if it had done nothing for me. This device I held in one hand as I placed it in Box 17 to put on Rack 64 was going out in the world to be part of important stories.

This PV721DVAB seatbelt in box number 18 would

be someone's safety. Someone's story concerning a close call, a tale that they might one day laugh about and tell at parties.

- Seatbelt 19 would be there the first time a sixteen-year-old got behind the wheel, making their parents slightly more comforted.
- Seatbelt number 20 and 21 will be there when two people have their first kiss. Creating an awkward moment of resistance as 20 and 21 hold them back.
- Number 22 will be sleek and smooth as someone deposits the down payment on their first car.
- Number 23 will be with someone as they drop off their kid on their first day at college, and will console them as they drive home alone.
- Number 24 will keep someone in their seat as they slam on the breaks from being distracted on their way to work.
- They will thank God for 24 and a second later they will forget about its existence.
- Just as I forget that number twenty-five will be part of numerous stories of safety, adventure, and life-altering moments.

As I place twenty-five in its box I don't look at it. I throw it in without a thought, as we so often treat those that are unfailingly kind to us. At the end of the day your body is no longer your own. You leave with the wrists of an eighty-year-old arthritic patient, Quasimodo's hump-back, and the tired feet of a marathon runner.

Sometimes at the end of the shift, exhausted and dirty and scratched up I will even hate seatbelt number 25.

Deus Ex Machina

Robert Earl Stewart

In the right-of-way, like ashes, the welders walk in the
snow
reconstituting slowly in the fog or mist
or smoke or gauze.

They're backlit by the arms of a many-armed mollusk
that cracks quietly into being, orange and arcing
but felt through the double glass like an underwater
break,

then burning out past black
to grey then a white that stands out against so much
white,
then veined with a black contrail and punctuated

with a small falling planet
through the wild carrot and goldenrod, and everything
else pelted with frost and by powder,

the essential blackness glowing underneath.
Some of them bend to their work; others set out
in the direction of the station,

slow enough to accommodate everything so briefly.
And we cannot tell what they're doing there, so suddenly
and slowly,

but they leave two-tone tracks,
their tread pressing down to the soot, like ghosts are
milling there,
misting opals around their boot prints, in the gauze,

the smoke, the mist, the fog.
And that's a very quiet second, in which I wonder
whether the train moves, or the city.

Crow-Filled Sky

Michael Schatte

The wife said won't you come your plate's getting cold.
No I said I'll watch this hell unfold
They're running round like horses licked by flame
I cringe and sigh and watch it all the same

Wolves in the street
Troops on their feet
And I've got a front-row seat

I try but I can't look away
I cry but I can't look away
I'll die but I can't look away
From the crow-filled sky

Cities burn as earthquakes shimmy and shake
Kingdoms fall as factions claim their stake
Pity all those who must be near the end
Aren't we thankful we've got CNN

The world's indiscreet
Ain't it a treat
And I've got a front row seat

I try but I can't look away
I cry but I can't look away
I'll die still I can't look away
From the crow-filled sky

Wallstreet melts and Mainstreet's on the dole
Fearful folk let terror take control
What of the future does the skyline show
We can't see for all these bloody crows

The law in retreat
Oncoming heat
And I've got a front row seat

I try but I can't look away
I cry but I can't look away
I'll die still I can't look away
From the crow-filled sky

I'll Give You No Conclusions

A Social Commentary on the Culture of Corruption in Cuba

Richard M. Grove

I have been to Cuba over fifteen times in the last 10 to 12 years. I love the country and the people and I plan on going back many more times as a tourist and with the Canada Cuba Literary Alliance, of which I am president. With all of this visiting and appreciation of the country for some reason, I had a bit of an eye opener this past trip that I am calling "the culture of corruption".

More than any trip in the past I noticed how much stealing from the government goes on. I am sure that this culture of cheating and stealing from the government has been growing slowly for many decades, but now it seems to have grown to mountainous proportions. Nothing this pervasive could possibly grow overnight. If for no other reason I am interested in this as a sociological phenomenon. What caused it and how did it get so out of hand?—if in fact it is as bad as I suggest. Even though it could not possibly be a new phenomenon I have just newly become aware of how pervasive it is. I am sure that most tourists and maybe even Cubans are not aware of just how this culture of corruption has fit into the everyday life of virtually every Cuban.

Let me start by saying that I am not suggesting that Cuba, as a nation, is morally bankrupt, but I am saying that stealing from the government is rampant. In Canada we all lock the doors to our houses and our cars. We chain our bicycles with "Kryptonite" locks; we watch our camera with an eagle's eye if we set it down and feel for our wallets if we are bumped in a crowd. I am not at all trying to wag the judgmental finger or condemn any one person. It is just that I am newly surprised by how deep and at the same time, close to the surface this culture of corruption is in Cuba. How did it happen and what are the consequences? The quick and obviously easy answer to "How did it happen" is poverty. Stealing for survival is a slippery slope; it trains the instincts of clever conniving.

One issue about theft that I have not looked at very deeply is the issue of one Cuban stealing from another Cuban. I do know that this kind of personal and maybe petty theft does occur, but to what extent I don't know. The bars on the windows of virtually every home make this evident, but I have a feeling that this type of personal theft is not as pervasive as theft from the government though I am willing to confess that I may be naive about this. It may be that the culture of stealing is an all pervasive fact of life and that stealing from a fellow Cuban is simply not as pervasive simply because your average Cuban does not have much of anything to steal. This may be an irony worth looking at some other time.

Is stealing from the government more pervasive merely because, aside from a few personal items, everything is owned and operated by the government? Stealing is not a foreign concept to us in Canada. In North America we know, only too well, the idiom—It fell off the back of a truck. Nothing ever falls off the back of the truck and if it did one has the choice of whether to keep it or buy it or not. Are morals ever an easy choice to make? Because of our high standard of living one might say that in Canada one has the choice as to whether or not to participate in corruption. Is it all that simple of an issue in Cuba? Is deprivation such a deep-rooted part of the culture that one has no choice other than to participate for the sake of survival? All I know is, that in Cuba, theft from the government is incredibly wide spread to the point that, dare I say, every individual is to some degree a willingly participant in this culture of corruption.

Is there just an individual or communal blind eye given to this culture of corruption or is it possible that it is so widespread that there is a governmental blind eye also? Is it possible for a Cuban to live without participating in such corruption? How have I, as a tourist, advertently or inadvertently participated in this corruption and how have I perhaps been duped by this dishonesty? I did not start off intending to compile a list of difficult questions. They simply formed as I mulled over what I have seen and experienced. None of these are easy questions to answer and I try to ponder these issues without judgment of any individual. I am in no position to judge anyone.

Let me give you a few simple examples of how stealing from the government is a norm in Cuba and is considered an innocent way of increasing one's income. I took a bicycle to Cuba this last trip. It was in a large box and I wondered just how difficult it was going to be for me to get this box to my casa particular where I was staying. I wheeled my luggage cart out of the terminal into the Cuban sun to find a cab. I was instantly offered a ride by an official, government-licensed cab driver behind the wheel of a small station wagon. I was delighted to have my problem so instantly solved. I asked him, up front, how much the ride would cost and he told me $10.00 Cuban Convertible Pesos = $10 USA. Without hesitation I seized the opportunity and we drove off in air-conditioned comfort and I was delivered in 10 or 15 minutes to my destination.

Because I had my bicycle I had no other need for a cab while there until I was heading back to the airport to come home. Martha, my casa hostess kindly called for a cab and told me that the ride would be $7.00 Cuban Convertible Pesos. Hmm, $3 less to go the same distance. Was this because it would be a smaller car I thought but no the same size station wagon arrived. When we arrived at the airport I noticed that the metre said $6.50. When I gave the driver a $10 note he said thank you, put it in his pocket, dashed my one piece of luggage into the airport and walked away. Was I duped by both drivers? Did I willingly or unwillingly participate in the culture of corruption? Should I have demanded my change and then offered the driver, a very nice man in both cases by the way, a tip? This is a pretty small example. Does it fall under the culture of corruption theme or should I have simply been more astute and diligent in paying the correct fee? In the first taxi the driver did not put the metre on and most likely pocketed the entire $10. For the second ride the driver had the metre on but slyly pocketed the $3.50 in hopes he would get away with a large tip—maybe 3 times larger than I might have offered him. In some ways both examples appear pretty harmless until you add up the amount of money. How many unregistered trips will that driver make in a day? 10? 10 X $10 = $100.00 Cuban Convertible Pesos from that one driver did not go to the Cuban government. How many days a week does that driver work? How many taxi drivers are doing the same thing across the country? Use your own imagination to come up with how many thousands upon thousands of pesos are not going to the government in a year and in the end not being fairly distributed to the population in the form of better food and housing. Is it justified because he thinks he is a victim of poverty?

A year or two ago I saw a bus driver with his head buried in work under the hood of his bus while the Cuban musicians, that he was the driver for, were playing in the shade on a public stage not very far away. Oh poor guy has to be out in the heat fixing the bus while the musicians are playing on a shaded stage, was my empathetic thought until it was pointed out to me that he was not fixing his bus. He was siphoning diesel fuel into two litre pop bottles and selling it as cooking fuel to the line of people beside his bus. I was shocked, he was stealing fuel from his bus and selling it. Clever? No, conniving.

You can bet this practice of selling fuel has been going on for a long time and with more than just this one driver. When something this cleverly conniving is being done so blatantly in the open you can bet it is common practice. He may cut the musicians in on the profit and maybe even his boss, I don't know, but this culture of corruption cannot be hidden very deep, it must be a common occurrence. Someone higher up must know that it is happening. Why is it tolerated?

How many drivers across the country are stealing fuel and selling it to line their own pockets—hundred, thousands? Stealing fuel and selling it to whom? Cuba is a Socialist, some would say Communist, country. From whom is he stealing it? From no other than the very people that he is selling it to—an interesting conundrum. I am starting to wonder if this culture of corruption is nothing more than a convoluted, corrupt distribution method covertly sanctioned by the government. Steal from yourself—you are the people and you are the state and then sell to yourself—you are the people and you are the state. Actually it is convoluted and sick. How many steps away is this survival method from the most primitive compassionless survival method of the biggest and the strongest survive. Not much different. The cleverly conniving survive, and the stupid and honest perish. Not a very idyllic environment to live in. It is a self-perpetuating cycle of corruption. You cannot afford to be stupid or honest.

Well let's go back to the airport for a few minutes. I got in line to check in. When I put my luggage on the scale the attendant said it was overweight by a few kg. I argued that my ticket said right on it that I was allowed more than he was telling me. Then I realized what was going on. He wanted me to offer him a bribe to make the problem go away. I overtly asked him "How much should the bribe be?"—he said $10. We dickered for a few minutes and arrived at $5.00. Then I said that I wanted to talk to his supervisor to ask his advise on just how much the bribe should be. I held up my hand and waved to his supervisor to come over. Instantly the attendant said because I am his amigo he would put my luggage through without charging me anything. How many dollars a day does he dupe from innocent tourists? Is it justifiable because he earns so little compared to me? Is it justifiable because he is not working in a job that has a legitimate tipping method? The price I paid for standing up for myself was that the customs inspector called my name over the airport intercom. When I arrived at his counter he insisted on inspecting my luggage even though I was leaving the country. He delayed me for 3/4 of an hour and dumped everything out for me to repack. Not a large price to pay, but it left me with a bad feeling.

Even though I have many similar experiences none of these examples seem very dramatic and worthy of labelling as a cultural phenomenon. Let's jump to something that has a much greater, less hidden, impact on Cuba and its citizens. While walking and talking with a Cuban friend one year I commented that the sidewalk all of a sudden became a dangerous potholed, crumbling mass of loose concrete. Why would that be when most of the sidewalks all around were in perfectly good shape, though after closer inspection I did realize that every so often I did find a sidewalk in very similar condition. It was suggested to me that the contractor, an employee of the state, was scrimping on the cement and selling it. A little too much sand, and a lot less cement makes for a sidewalk that will crumble within six or eight months. The inspection process would have been done months before the crumbling and the contractor would have pocketed and spent the profit from the sale of the missing cement long ago.

My friend then told me that he, at one time, had purchased concrete that—fell off the back of the truck. The irony of ironies is that he had hired a contractor to use some stolen concrete in a building project that soon started to fall apart because there was not enough cement in the mix. He then had to scramble to fix the problem by purchasing more cement that—fell off the back of the truck. Victim, victimizer—what goes around comes around. It is not just a matter of being smart enough not to get caught, or smart enough to make sure that your contractor uses the right amount of cement. The point is that the culture of corruption does have the victim / victimizer axiom built into it no matter how hidden. On a spiritual level one is proving the axiom of victim / victimizer every time one participates in the culture of corruption. The problem is that when you enact the axiom of victim / victimizer it will rear its head and bite you one day. No one is so smart or fast enough to not become the victim one day. Thinking back to the sidewalk I wondered at the time if anyone had ever fallen and been hurt because of the crumbling sidewalk. Consequence—every action has a consequence. Do you dare believe that wrong actions have bad consequences?

Let me give you another simple example of how I have inadvertently participated in this culture of corruption. One night I asked the bartender if he sold bags of coffee like the large one that he used to make the wonderful cappuccinos with. I had been downtown Havana and seen the exact brand and size of bag in a store for $9.50. Not too bad of a price considering the quality and size of bag, but I had neglected to purchase one as a gift. When I was offered one for $6.50 I snapped it up. It was not until the bartender surreptitiously slipped it into my bag, when no one was looking, that I realized that I had just been party to corruption even if only on a small level. Should

I have instantly, insistently, demanded my money back. I did not have enough time to think. I walked away pondering what had just transpired. In hindsight I regret having purchased the coffee that fell off the back of the truck.

How many bags of coffee does he sell in a day, a week, a year? Yes it is lining his pocket, but what this, otherwise fine, gentleman is not thinking about is how this corruptive transaction is going to affect the bottom line of the government—in effect his fellow Cubans let alone the spiritual bottom line of himself. This culture of corruption does have ramifications that go deeper than money. The spiritual ramifications are far more important.

A MUCH WATERED LAWN

John B. Lee

"for the love of money is the root of all evil" – Timothy

"Money must not lie about value. It must not, by inflation or usury, misrepresent the value of necessary work or necessary goods. Those values must not, by any devices of markets or banks, be made subject to monetary manipulation." – First law of economics from the Essay "Fallacies" by Wendell Berry

"A cynic is a man who knows the price of everything and the value of nothing." – Oscar Wilde

"What a terrible enemy the desperate want of money is for the achievement of virtues!" – José Martí

"You can measure a man's intelligence by how long it takes him in conversation before he begins talking of money." – Herbert Mercer Lee

Most days I shave a stranger. I see his soul shining out from silver glass. Indeed, if I lean in close, his spirit smells of glass. His face hangs over the sink like a painting caught in the glorious light of morning. Somewhere deep inside he is the same fellow he ever was. He vanishes when I look away. He disappears in the dark. When I am not there, it seems, he is not there. Still, in our mutual absence, he might be more present as we are sometimes more present in the presence of absence. If we listen in the quiet, he might be overheard to be saying in silence true self to true self:

"Hello there lost youth."

"Greetings, old codger."

• • •

My father loved to amuse children by demonstrating the casting out of nines and then asking the question, "Why does it work?"

The casting out of nines is a lovely and elegant example of a pattern occurring when one observes the consequences of adding the digits resulting from the multiplication of the number nine.

9 X 1 = 9	9 + 0 = 9
9 X 2 = 18	1 + 8 = 9
9 X 3 = 27	2 + 7 = 9
9 X 4 = 36	3 + 6 = 9
9 X 5 = 45	4 + 5 = 9
9 X 6 = 54	5 + 4 = 9
9 X 7 = 63	6 + 3 = 9
9 X 8 = 72	7 + 2 = 9
9 X 9 = 81	8 + 1 = 9
9 X 10 = 90	9 + 0 = 9

and so on ...

Dad loved this demonstration and he loved to amuse children who responded to his question, "Why does it work?" by saying either nothing, or by saying "I don't know," or by saying, "Show me again."

But I was a strange lad. I frustrated my father's party trick by responding, "Dad, you're asking the wrong question."

He didn't really know what to make of me then. It wasn't that I hadn't been amazed. It was that I had made something entirely different out of the demonstration of the casting out of nines. I wanted him to say to me, "What do you mean? What question should I be asking, then?" And he had wanted me to be one in a crowd of amazed children. We neither of us played our parts well.

He wanted to be the magus of the casting out of nines. I wanted to be the one who saw to the centre of a conundrum. To him, I had pulled the curtain on the wizard. I longed for the fascination of a deeper amazement. I sought clarity of thought rather than certainty of conviction. "Why does it work?" led me to say, "It works because it works."

I wanted my father to ask the question, "What is it?"—meaning—"What is the phenomenon you call *the casting out of nines?*" The answer to this question in my mind would prove far more interesting.

So finally, after years of frustration my father acquiesced and said, "Okay, what question should I be asking?" I tell him. And then I go on.

"Dad," I say, "the casting out of nines is an elegant and recurring pattern peculiar to the number nine. This phenomenon is an observation of a pattern, not the invention of a pattern. It is a discovery, not a creation. And as such it is evidence of the fact that we humans have a predilection for observing patterns. It is in our nature to see *in* nature that which we are predisposed to seeing. It is this predisposition that led Einstein to conclude, "God does not play dice with the universe." This same love for classical mathematics led Lewis Carroll to pose the unanswerable riddle, "Why is a raven like a writing desk?" as a satire of the chaos infecting late-nineteenth century mathematics, and it also gives rise to an admiration for the elegance of *the casting out of nines.*

The answer to my father's question "Why does it work?" is entirely tautological. It works because it works. It works because it exists. The answer to the question "How does it work?" is in the demonstration. That too is a closed circle. One might admire the way it works as one admires the beauty of a six-sided snowflake or a four-fingered hand. One might well ask, "How is a snowflake?" or "Why is a snowflake?" And one might find a fascinating metaphysics in the sophistry of exploring such a question. But as for me, I wanted to dwell on the *whatness of the thing* before plunging beyond the thing itself. As poet William Carlos Williams once stated, "No ideas but in things."

We can observe. We can name. We can modify and deepen and clarify for a more reliable observation. We can leap into the real. We cannot comprehend that which is beyond our understanding. We cannot help but plod within the limitations of our limited cognition. We cannot see the unseeable, hear the unhearable, touch the untouchable, taste the untasteable, smell the unsmellable. We are physical beings. We are children of time. If in the hierarchy of being we sometimes characterize ourselves as the apex animal, we must acknowledge the fact that as I wrote in my poem, "Teaching My Dog to Read: the first lesson":

Pool hall, Beeton, Ontario *(M.G.)*

Corktown, Detroit *(M.G.)*

Parking lot booth, Windsor *(M.G.)*

Detroit *(M.G.)*

Ambassador Bridge, winter *(M.G.)*

Abandoned factory *(M.G.)*

Move In Now *(M.G.)*

Downtown mission, Detroit *(M.G.)*

Woodward Avenue, Detroit *(M.G.)*

Waiting for the bus, Detroit *(M.G.)*

Shady Motel, now torn down, St. Joachim *(M.G.)*

Diner, Detroit *(M.G.)*

Meal, Trappist monastery, Kentucky *(M.G.)*

Rooms for Rent *(M.G.)*

what we cannot see
with our eyes
hawks see
what we cannot hear
with our ears
owls hear
what we cannot smell
with our noses
dogs smell
what we cannot feel
with our flesh
butterflies feel
what we cannot taste
with our tongues
snakes taste
and this is the moon
in the womb
the stone in the centre of sleep
the red
that we draw from a dream
the ribbon of life
in the light of old tides
where what's deep
as a heart in the dark
with you palm to the bone of the breast
you might touch
what the hand
cannot hold.

I think it is obvious that the god of geese is a goose and the god of gulls a gull. So too, we might acknowledge that the dog in the library is the only one who sees the ghost in the doorway. He does not know himself to be in the thick of meaning as it is written in the record of human history in the books that surround him. We who know the entire works of Shakespeare by heart may be humbled by the olfactory knowledge of a fox terrier too lively and dogsome to learn to read.

The man in the mirror was conceived a poet in the womb and born a poet in a room. He was lucky enough to be able to live a life that lead to becoming what he always was. If Plato was correct about education, then all learning is recollection. All study is the study that reminds us of the things we have always known. Education is the work of memory. Deep waters want only a clear light. Insight is the seeing of that which has ever been there. Profound revelation is reliable observation. Knowledge is truth made real.

Now like the dull man of my grandfather's caveat, I turn my thoughts to original purpose, a contemplation of the meaning of money. And as it was with the casting out of nines, I ask first questions first. Not 'How does money work?" Not "Why does money exist?" But rather, I ask myself, "What is money?" And at first blush I have to confess that I don't really know. I do know that without money, in this culture, at this point in history, I am at the mercy of the fates. I cannot participate in the culture at large. Without money I have no food. The moneyless man is without shelter in the cold of winter, without clothing in an unforgiving climate that kills the naked man. Without money I am not myself. I am someone else's self. I am the doomed mendicant. I am the lost penurious beggar with my hand open to the rain and the fickle charity of others. This was not such a problem for the child, because the child found himself nurtured by his parents. Like a fledgling, I fled the nest and sought my own way in the world. One need I discovered very early was the need for money. What is this thing I needed? What is *money*?

The Story of Stone Money

All my life, when I have thought of it at all, I have wondered about the story of stone money. Since when I had first heard of it as I schoolboy, I had been curious as to why and how a culture would choose to make its money from stone. I had wrongly imagined a people simply stooping down and gathering up granite, shaping that dross into wheels of coin, and with that rubbled-up currency heavy enough to necessitate the boring through of a centre hole then thrusting through a shaft, and with the carry-weight of a two-man burden, a duel of porters lugging stone money through the jungle to the marketplace for the purchase price of a vendor's wares, just as I might carry a nickel in my hand to the confectioner's counter for a five-cent bag of penny candy or drop a dime in the offertory as a child's tithe in a Sunday pew. I could not imagine the rock-ribbed agora of an ancient people without wondering how the geology of their currency worked. Why not simply bend down and scoop up a fistful of gravel just there as you arrive at the point of sale and drop that screed in the merchant's hand and go home whistling like any old happy jack with your newly purchased billy goat trailing on his rope. Surely there is something to this story of stone money that I do not get. And so, the time has come for me to ask—*what is stone money*?

At first blush, and without detail, it seems a dumb coinage, dumb beyond doing the work that money does, for money *is* a metaphor. Everyone involved in the story of money must agree that this particular piece of paper, this particular minted copper, this exacting black-line ledger, this merchant's talisman, this nation's talent *has* value, either by the spectacular glint in the jeweller's eye, or by the stamped face of a famous general, official prince, common panjandrum, elected mugwump, assassinated president, or anachronistic queen, either that or by the wheelbarrow load of a failing people's green-ink paper, as in times of plenty a pig-in-a-poke smoke-and-mirrors Ponzi scheme or a smart-man's greedy scam, imaginary wheat, next-year's corn, or nothing-at-all accident of a defeated confederacy—what is *money?*—but a lie agreed upon.

King Midas goes hungry with his golden spoon. His alchemy starves the rich. His wife's a wealthy dust. His wine's a sip of greed. His children gilded by a sweet embrace, each one's become statuary bullion frozen by his touch. What's Aaron's calf to him?—a fool's delight, an empty wish, the pyrite of an idiot's last dream.

I need to know the story of stone money.

There was an island long ago and far away in space and time—an isolated island, remote and lonesome in the waves of the western Pacific. That island known as Yap had a king who sent his men seafaring far and wide. On the island of Palau they found a rare and shiny rock. This they quarried and brought home. They called this glittering rock Rai and made it their money. These large donut-shaped, carved disks of calcite are sometimes up to four meters in diameter though most are much smaller. The lift-weight of the largest coin requires the labour of twenty adult men. The Yapese valued these disks because they were the shiniest objects around. The stones became legal tender and were even mandatory in some payments.

The stones' value was kept high due to the hazard involved in obtaining them. To quarry the stones, Yapese adventurers had to sail to distant islands and deal with local inhabitants who were sometimes hostile. Once quarried, the disks had to be transported back to Yap on rafts towed behind wind-powered canoes. The scarcity of the disks, and the effort and peril required to get them, made them valuable to the Yapese. However, in 1874, an enterprising Irishman named David O'Keefe hit upon the idea of employing the Yapese to import more money in the form of shiploads of large stones, also from Palau. O'Keefe then traded these stones with the Yapese for other commodities such as sea cucumbers and copra. Although some of the O'Keefe stones are larger than the canoe-transported stones, they are less valuable than the earlier stones due to the comparative ease with which they were obtained. Approximately 6,800 of them are scattered around the island. Thus the stone economy collapsed. Now the people of the island use the United States dollar for currency though the stone money remains valued and is sometimes passed from generation to generation on the occasion of a marriage or at a time of death.

First Things

I wrote my very first poem when I was eight years old. I composed it at school as a verse to place within a Father's Day card we were called upon to make as an art project. I was not impressed by the options written on the blackboard by the teacher and presented for our consideration as something that might honour our individual fathers. On the front fold of my offering, I drew a green-screen console television set much like the one in our very own parlour on the farm. Inside, I dedicated my card *To a Fried* having accidentally elided the 'n' of the intended word "friend." "To a Friend" was indeed a common enough greeting-card salutation as to make it seem natural and appropriate to a boy who did not know any better. To this flimsy work of art I taped a six-sided nickel as a gift amounting to a denomination that I could afford and which to me seemed an extravagance certain to be appreciated not only by any father, but also by my father in particular.

I can only wonder now, what I must have imagined then, what my father might have purchased with this precious five-cent coin: five jaw breakers, a plastic bag of cat's eye marbles, a single try at the crane arcade, a bag of chips, a chocolate bar, a comic book, a spider ring in a bubble gum machine, a single box of pink elephant popcorn, sponge toffee, an hour at the parking meter in Detroit City, five thoughts at a penny each, or maybe something for me.

In reality he did not spend the nickel, but saved it all his life. He saved that nickel till the tape cracked and the glue gave way. He preserved that green TV until the crayon faded and paper yellowed with age. He laughed a full-bellied laugh to show family and friends, not only because it revealed how his son had loved him as a child. He drew the onlooker's attention to the phrase "To a Fried" as the nickel caused the page to droop like a rain-wet lily.

What then is the meaning of money in this tale? What does it reveal about the child?

One of my personal favourites of my father's jokes goes like this. Dad is sitting at the head of the table where the seven of us are seated for family dinner. He announces, "I bought a twenty thousand dollar dog today."

"A twenty thousand dollar dog?"

"Yes, a twenty thousand dollar dog."

"How's that?"

"Yes. I bought a twenty thousand dollar dog. I traded two ten-thousand dollar cats for him."

And however many times he told this joke I always laughed and took his meaning.

A Much Watered Lawn

My Canadian friends who water their grass in the interest of producing a green lawn often bemuse me. As my farmer uncle once said of a pasture being burned off in order to plow the ash into the soil, "95% of the humus is in the earth." This deep green achieved by the aforementioned watering creates the appearance of healthy grass, but this watering encourages green growth above the earth all the while it discourages the deepening of the roots. The water-green grass is actually very precarious and exceptionally susceptible to disease and insect infestation because the roots do not go very deep.

Far better to let the surface go brown and wait for rain, for the browning of the grass encourages root development and when the rain arrives the grass comes back quickly and in that it is deeply rooted, it is far healthier than much-watered grass.

The use of pesticides and herbicides which make it a toxic and glamorous destructive monoculture also pamper the much-watered lawn of know-nothing and couldn't care-less lawn-growing folk. In this way bright-green falsely healthy grass resembles popular culture where wealth and fame take precedence over substance and Hollywood looks trump talent. One of the major psychological sicknesses of North American popular culture involves our fascination with celebrity culture and our addiction to the twin poisons of mass-market youth culture, unearned wealth and no-talent fame. Midas and Narcissus are the two most tragic fools of Greek mythology, the former addicted to gold, the latter fascinated by personal beauty.

It is also interesting to note that an imam living in the United States maintained that the greatest sin in America is the sin of the American lawn. Imagine dream-green lawns in the deserts of Nevada, Arizona, Texas and New Mexico. So much water is stolen and diverted for the luxury of building cities in the desert that the Colorado does not make it to the sea, but rather it dries up and vanishes into inland arroyos in Mexico. Imagine that! This great river, which carved out the Grand Canyon, fails to reach the ocean.

Poetry, visual arts, and certain kinds of performing arts such as troubadour culture exist and indeed to a certain degree thrive in the absence of money. I am not suggesting for a moment that they are encouraged by poverty. Creative arts are produced by committed artists motivated by the need to write, sing, paint, draw, compose, perform even in the absence of monetary reward. Those committed artists are often quite poor and living well below the poverty line in the nation they call home. The commoditization of the arts and what poet Wendell Berry refers to as "the fever chart of consumption" lend themselves to the commoditization of the soul—a world where Mozart is thrown in a pauper's grave and madness and penury drive Van Gogh to suicide and despair. Poets, if they exist in the marketplace at all, are relegated to the kick-plate region of the bookstore.

A Diner for the Dead

There is a diner in the city where I used to live. Photographs and paintings of the icons of popular culture decorate the walls in the restaurant. With only two exceptions every famous individual represented there is dead. Most of them died tragically. This brings to mind the often-quoted maxim of the sixties, "Live fast. Die young. Make a beautiful corpse." When the waitress came to take my order, I said to her in a mischievous tone, "I see dead people," quoting a line from the movie *Sixth Sense*.

She showed almost no interest in my concern. I pressed on. "Did you notice that of all the people portrayed on your walls there are only two who are currently living? Can you tell me who those two are?"

She wanted a tip, so she played along. "No. Who

are they?" She inquired with the perfunctory concern of someone wanting my money.

She glanced around and I listed the dead: "James Dean died in a car crash; Elvis died on the toilet; Jim Morrison died in a bath tub in Paris; Marilyn Monroe committed suicide in a bed in L.A.; Jimi Hendrix aspirated on his own vomit in an apartment in London; Janis Joplin died of a heroin overdose; Jane Mansfield was decapitated; John Lennon was shot by a madman in New York City; George Harrison was stabbed in the lung by an intruder and then died a few years later of throat cancer; aren't they beautiful, famous, wealthy, forever young, eternally dead and gone?"

When she gives up I reveal to her that of all the people on the walls of the diner only Paul McCartney and Ringo Starr remain among the living.

The sad fact is that she remains unimpressed and it seems she could not care less.

I wonder about the health of a culture that embraces Thanatos as if it were Eros. Wasn't it Joseph Goebbels who said, "Whenever I hear the word *culture*, I reach for my gun"?

Actually that line comes from a 1933 play by Hans Jost. But then who am I to quarrel with Goebbels? Who am I, indeed?

Tyler's Tale

My wife tells me I am wrong about this. She says the waitress is simply doing her job, working hard, serving the public. "It's not that she doesn't care to know, it's that she's far too busy to care to know," Cathy says. "That waitress just wants to take your order and get on with her duties. You're being far too clever."

Then after she reads what I've written thus far, she reminds me of a story involving a child she once taught. This is Tyler's Tale. These are her memories of him. This is one memory she tells me she wishes she could leave behind.

The first time she saw Tyler, he was waiting on the steps of the mould-infested portable classroom she had just been assigned. It was the hottest day of September and Tyler was dressed for the new school year. Clothed in an oversized Chicago Bulls winter coat with a backpack humped on his shoulders, it was immediately obvious that someone loved him enough to ensure that he show up on the first day in brand-new duds. Unfortunately the brand-new winter coat revealed that some loving guardian had sent him out into the world without a care or concern for the sun beating down on his hot little frame cooking his eager body till his cheeks burned red. He didn't seem to mind. He was proud of that coat and possessive of the contents of his pack.

It was always a challenge to get him to slouch out of his backpack and to remove his coat when the bell rang in order to persuade him that it would be far easier to participate in activities of the day unencumbered by coat and pack. Even getting him to take it off simply to sit in the desk was a daunting task. The days turned into weeks, the weeks into months and the coat got dirtier and dirtier with wear. The straps on the cheap backpack stretched with use and eventually broke under the strain of the weight of the things he carried. Five novels earned as library prizes, games he'd been given by Santa Claus, new socks and mitts donated by a parent who worked at a local dry-goods store, Easter colouring books, everything he owned it seemed, went into the back pack and he lugged it around like a refugee.

Every day at lunch he took what appeared to be a horse-pill worth of medication prescribed by his doctor because in the doctor's professional medical opinion he was "an aggressive child prone to outbursts of rage leading to probability if not certainty of physical violence."

As the year wore on winter came and went, and cool spring days turned into warm spring days and the heat and humidity gave rise to body odor and the stink of unwashed clothing it came time to sanitize the belongings of each student. Every child emptied their bag and we disposed of soggy potato chip crumbs, wet homework, long-forgotten items and in some cases wet winter boots or woollen mittens. In Tyler's case we discovered what he had been carrying with him all year long. Hiding deep inside his bag he carried his uneaten lunch. The lunch he carried, it seemed, was the same lunch he had brought with him that first day when I'd met him waiting on the steps of the classroom.

When I attempted to throw the rancid food into the trash he became very agitated. His mother had packed his lunch that first day. She was poor and could barely afford the groceries she bought. Whenever he did not eat his lunch, he was required to bring home the uneaten food. He was then required to eat it for supper or go hungry. The next day, she repacked the uneaten lunch in his backpack. The cycle repeated itself all year. The food became stale. Then it became moldy. Then it began to rot. Then it became rancid and runny, liquid and fragrant with horrible maggoty stink of spoiled meat and rotten fruit. Because of the drugs he was on he had no appetite and he'd kept himself alive by eating the treats offered by others and by snacking on the free food provided twice a week by the parents' council.

By the end of the school year his coat was still two sizes too large. He had not grown a centimetre. Despite phone calls and pleas for help, the system refused to intercede on his behalf. There was of course much hand wringing and expression of concern. However, in the ensuing September he was transferred to a new school and so he became someone else's problem.

On the last day of June, he wriggled away from my goodbye hug. He knew I had done my best to help him. He knew that there would be others who would do their best as well. Perhaps this was all he could hope for.

"When I think about him now, I can honestly say, that I cannot remember a single occasion when I ever saw him smile." Cathy said. "Write about him. Perhaps knowing his story might make you return to the drawing board."

I think here of the comedian's ironic words. "It's not the despair. I can take the despair. It's the hope I can't stand."

And I do not laugh at this thought. Not this time.

A FINAL THOUGHT

A knowledge of and appreciation for irony may be the only true measure of intelligence, but for just this little while, I'm done with irony. I want the true sentiment of a caring and empathetic heart. I want a government of compulsory compassion.

In this essay I have been wrestling with the meaning of money. I have been suggesting that all too often we have been asking ourselves the wrong questions. We have been focusing our attention on the wrong problems.

I can tell you now, that if we are condemned to live in a world where the wealth that exists *is* defined by the word money, then I want not for us to love money, but rather for money to love us. The wind and the water love us all the same. The sky and the sun and the moon and the stars love us all the same. Why not imagine a world where wealth loves humanity? Otherwise you can have it. However you define it. Whatever you call it. It hates us all the same.

And perhaps when my mother misquotes the Bible saying, "Money is the root of all evil," she is actually coming closer to the truth than I'm willing to admit.

The Seesaw

Duane Tucker

"So the darkness shall be the light, and the stillness the dancing." – T.S. Eliot

"God turns you from one feeling to another and teaches by means of opposites, so that you will have two wings to fly, not one." – Rumi

I used to walk around looking for the light, demanding it appear. I'd drink gallons of coffee, force myself to write into the wee hours, trying to wring it out of myself, my surroundings. It took a severe illness to teach me that, often, the best stuff is lurking in the dark. I need to be patient: slip roots deep into the loam and wait for the greyish light to seep up into me. I need to take my time, look more deeply. Easy Does It.

The dark is a trickster, a shaman. There he sprawls in the smog of pain—fists clenched, eyes smouldering, proffering noxious potions. I force myself to sit with him. After a while, I notice that he's not smirking, but sulking from years and years of being misunderstood.

And those clenched fists? They're soft, pliable. I coax them open. They're full of seeds: despairs and angers, frustrations and disappointments. He's been moistening them; they're sprouting emerald tendrils. That dwindling bank account is sending down a filigree of the finest green. The shattered relationship is apriled with buds. And I see that he is the Buddha-bellied nothingness, the void that wombs the world.

There's an old Hindu parable about a guru who one day begins throwing stones at his students. Most of them are rattled. They flee the monastery, convinced their teacher has lost his mind. But the intuitive ones take the stones home, crack them open and discover gold inside.

How do we mine the gold in the boulders of the current economic downturn? How do we embrace painful change? Either life has meaning or it doesn't. If it does, then all circumstances arrive bearing gifts. The great saint Sister Guynamata used to pray, "Change no circumstance in my life. Change me." In other words, help me learn the lesson.

Meanwhile, what about the pain? In the big picture, I do my best look at it as the quick sting of the Great Physician's needle injecting me with growth hormones. Or the hand of God passing between me and the sun as it moves down to bless.

Still, it smarts like hell. So I write. What a wonderful anodyne: two silences embracing each other across the raging abyss of time and space—enriching each with music and aroma and spice.

How uplifting to take to the woods on a lonely day and have a sunbeam whisper to you, a pebble give you a smile. Even more healing to take the smile to your desk and broaden it; amplify the whisper to a song. And then to see the smile in the reader as they hear it!

Is it any wonder so many doctors became writers? William Carlos Williams was a doctor. Chekhov as well. The list goes on: Schiller, Maugham, Conan Doyle, Keats, Rabelais, Oliver Wendell Holmes. Perhaps their

Ford City, Windsor *(M.G.)*

Detroit *(M.G.)*

Abandoned parking lot, Detroit *(M.G.)*

Homeless mural *(M.G.)*

Parking lot for Tiger Stadium *(M.G.)*

Airport workers *(M.G.)*

Old lady and photos *(M.G.)*

Bakery *(M.G.)*

Abandoned factory *(M.B.)*

Clothespins *(M.G.)*

Stop the worry *(M.G.)*

Car lot in winter *(M.G.)*

Books *(S.S.P.)*

Sunset *(M.G.)*

affinity for the healing arts, prompted a desire to heal deeper wounds.

It's been said that wounds are blessings in disguise: beckonings to reach beyond our self-absorbed boundaries into the sunrise of altruism. Darkness and light can and should nourish each other. Some primitive cultures believe that they would fall over without their shadow. It's the thing that holds them up, keeps them going. Perhaps they have a point: My gut pain forces me to rivet my attention in the third eye to dispel it. My real eyes are going, forcing me to look more within—same with the ears. My thinning memory serves to thicken the present. The blackest periods in my life have produced the shiniest stuff.

• • •

One morning in 1983 I began writing a play loosely based on my volunteer experiences in nursing homes. At dawn—eighteen hours, a dozen cups of coffee and a fistful of vitamins later—I brought the curtain down. Never before or since have I had a similar burst of creative energy. I felt wrung out and wonderful.

I tried for years to shape it, but it was beyond unruly—and into the proverbial drawer it went. A decade later, vacationing with my girl friend in Big Sur, California, exhausted from the aforementioned illness, I lay down next to a stream and fell asleep. I never napped before I got sick. I considered it a weakness.

I hadn't thought about the play in ages. Wasn't working on it. Wasn't planning to. But right there in the dirt, a dream tiptoed in with the solution. Unsolicited. Unexpected. Some might say random—but as 'ol Albert famously remarked, "God does not play dice with the universe."

In any event, there it was. The fix! I'd succumbed to the "darkness", and the answer I'd been driving myself batty over for a decade had calmly presented itself .

I'd been guided by a dream only once before: shortly after I contracted the illness. Chances for recovery in stressful, smog-ridden L.A. were slim, so I headed for the Sierra Nevada Mountains: surely the altitude and fresh air would help. It was a grim trip. I was incapacitated. I knew I'd have to quit acting, and the prospects of finding a new profession, in my condition, at my age were beyond dim.

• • •

One night, about 4 a.m., I awoke in the middle of a dream. I realized that it had been pestering me for some time, urging me to write something on John Muir, the poet, mystic, crusading environmentalist. Muir had roamed these mountains for years. The Muir Trail which threads the spine of the Sierra was a few miles from where I was staying. Had the illness driven me to Muir's back yard to connect with the dream?

It changed my life completely. I wrote a movie about Muir's crusade to preserve Yosemite. It was optioned. Excellent, perhaps I had found a way out of my dilemma! But like so many interesting projects in Hollywood, it ended up in the "round file".

I decided to write a one-man play. I'd perform it myself. The week I finished it, a woman whom I'd met in Mexico years earlier called out of the blue. She fell in love with the piece, and became the producer. We travelled around America and England with it. Business blossomed into romance. I married her and moved to Canada.

Every illness carries the seeds of the cure. Mine led me to my wife and profound rejuvenation as a Canadian. What a relief to be free of smogged-out, solipsistic L.A. It bonded me to Muir, who though terribly ill most of his life, never gave in to it. He founded the Sierra Club and convinced President Roosevelt to preserve Yosemite as a National Park.

The annals of creativity brim with dreams. Robert Louis Stevenson claimed many of his ideas arrived in dreams. Guiseppe Tartini wrote his masterpiece for the violin, the *Devil's Sonata*, after hearing it performed in a dream. Niels Bohr, dreaming of the way horses run at the race track, had an insight into how electrons remain in orbit. It became the basis for his quantum theory for which he was awarded a Nobel Prize. The Beatles' hit "Yesterday" was dream-born, as was Coleridge's "Kublai Khan".

Brahms was stuck on the second movement of his Romantic Symphony, when a conductor in black tie appeared to him in a dream and told him that it was ready. He should get up and play it. He did and there it was fully formed!

• • •

Two stabs at healing, two surrenders to "darkness"—the escape to the mountains, the nap in Big Sur—had yielded two dreams. But it was to take another, more nightmarish descent to fertilize the nursing home dream. For years I'd kept trying to rewrite the play with the dream in mind—but each time the efforts sputtered. I had no idea what was wrong. Maybe the dream was bogus. Maybe it still wasn't time. Maybe I'd never figure it out.

I drew comfort from the knowledge that Rilke had to wait fifteen years for the rest of the Duino Elegies. The first part had been dictated (by angels according to him) on the seashore near the Duino Castle—but it took a decade and a half for them to show up with the rest.

Recently—fifteen years after the dream!—my wife insisted on a separation. I was devastated. I'd never been married before, never even gotten close. She was the one! I'd been so sure I'd given up my beachfront place in Santa Monica, and committed my savings to buying an exquisite condo overlooking the Dundas Conservation Area. Bad enough the rift was shattering emotionally, but I was in dire straits financially. My teaching job had been cut back to one class.

Yet in the midst of the stress, all of a sudden, the play began to take shape. I wrote a draft in a month or so; and am, at this writing, feverishly revising. It appears that after more than a quarter of a century, I've finally broken through. I can't explain it any other way than intense suffering produces intense compensations.

The nightmare also goaded me to seek out another actor to perform the Muir piece. I'd long since discovered that I was far too ill to perform the Muir piece, and had abandoned it.

It wasn't long before a fabulously talented Stratford star came on board. I'm convinced he can take the piece to heights I never could, and finally give Muir his due. Muir was as famous in his day as Emerson and Thoreau, but for some reason history has developed amnesia, just when the planet needs his voice the most.

Here in my one bedroom apartment in Dundas, I'm undergoing a period of "monastic" discipline. It's hard times, but I'm buoyed by the notion that poverty is an ancient spiritual discipline, embraced by all the great souls. The more I diminish this world, the wider I open the door to the other. Poverty didn't do too badly by St. Francis, or Dostoyevsky or Joyce. Muir himself was poor for much of his life.

As Thoreau said, "Simplify, simplify, simplify! ... We are happy in proportion to the things we can do without.... Most of the luxuries, and many of the so-called comforts of life, are not only not indispensable, but positive hindrances to the elevation of mankind. With respect to luxuries and comforts, the wisest have even lived a more simple and meagre life than the poor."

I'm reminded of Mark Twain's dictum that no one is saved after the first twenty minutes of a sermon, so I'm going to wrap up.

The truly interesting aspect of living in duality is that we can be darn sure there is not a scrap of darkness without an equal amount of light attached to it. I call it the seesaw: if one side's down, the other's gotta be up. In other words, every recession has an equal and opposite accession.

As it turns out this recession may be my biggest boon, just as the illness has proven to be my greatest teacher. If I had to pinpoint the critical lesson I need learn in this life, it would have to be: "Easy Does It". The illness has force fed me a PHD—demanded I slow down, take long walks in the woods, let the big city springs unwind. And with each stride I make in the right direction, it backs off. I've learned that if the light's not easy, it's not ready; that even though I think I'm in charge of the process, it's doing most of the heavy lifting for me. It's a harsh teacher to be sure: at times squeezing me so tightly I can scarcely breathe—but I know exactly what it's doing: pythoning my true being to the surface.

So what if it's bleeding. It's bleeding flowers.

5

TOUGH TIMES STRAINING MARRIAGE

R.D. Roy

– In response to Mr. Harper's attempt to scare Canadians into thinking that the opposition's coalition with Quebec's elected representatives will 'destroy democracy in Canada'.

We are all the children of an uncommon union.

A child of France was made to marry, under threat of death, the cliff-climbing offspring of a conquering England. One imperial nation had just invaded the outpost of another imperial nation, and the resulting history is an example to the world.

The new husband was capable of a grace and intelligence seldom seen among nations, then or now, allowing the reluctant bride to keep her culture; her language, her church, her customs, and much of her commerce. Her deliberate assimilation was not pursued, and her own nature continued to flourish.

It is also possible that he recognized her brave determination and her beauty, and was willing to associate himself, to some extent, with those qualities.

This was a compromise and a promise the like of which a marriage is made, and with the grandparent's agenda notwithstanding, the couple have made a pretty good go of it.

This uncommon marriage of distinct nations has shown an enviable fidelity through the bitter and tragic winter of several wars abroad and an autumn crisis at home. And over the centuries there have been many lean decades which they have come through together, their agreement made stronger in the process.

Is the union idyllic? No, but what union really is?

From time to time the husband is heard to rant on her independent ways, on her repressed flirtation with freedom. And when she is chaffed within the house they share, she is known to mutter the odd curse in French.

And when she speaks her native tongue there is no truer way of understanding her.

One must wonder, in the great scheme of things, why it is only the wife that sometimes contemplates divorce. Though the women of the world would not need this aspect of a relationship to be explained!

It was conquest, of the military type, that wed them. Not love. And that inequity must forever be ignored by an act of will on her part.

So they remain married these two. Married in every sense of the word I can think of. In their maturity they have shown less wise nations and individuals what is possible.

They are bound now by choice, the good with the bad as any marriage must be, and we are all their confused and much loved children.

Swervings of the Heart

James Clarke

When my wife Mary and I got married in 1961, the future looked golden. She gave up a promising career as a fashion illustrator to raise a family. I pursued a law career that culminated in my appointment to the bench in 1983. Our children were happy, healthy and bright. We enjoyed many of the "good things" in life. In 1985 family and friends gathered at the local church to help us celebrate the renewal of our marriage vows. We considered ourselves lucky.

On April 8, 1990, a sunny Palm Sunday afternoon, everything changed. That was the day the police came to our door and dropped their bomb. My wife of 28 years had jumped to her death at Niagara Falls.

Several witnesses observed her climb the parapet of the observation platform, camera in her right hand, drop her shoulder purse to the ground and holding her nose (she always pinched her nose before plunging into water) leap into the Niagara River, floating on her back, eyes open, blank expression on her face, no struggle or cries till the strong current swept her over the rim of the Falls eleven stories down into the icy gorge below. Her body has never been found.

The foundation of my existence collapsed. Even to this day almost two decades later, my children and I still feel the aftershock.

Why, I asked. What could I have done differently?

For a long time after her suicide I wrestled with the question: what does God mean when a good person takes their life? I grew acutely aware of God's absence and the unfairness that runs through all of life like a fault line. Inside I was tender and raw. Not long after Mary's death a young woman appeared in my court. She testified that her husband hanged himself from a beam in the basement of their home. Instantly her words unleashed a flash flood of emotion that drove me from the courtroom, tears in my eyes.

Remorse and confusion led me to seek answers. I immersed myself in Carl Jung, began to track my dreams. Every morning I journalled on the computer-a form of free-association therapy. I strove to come to grips with what had happened.

Then, in the summer of 1995, visiting an aunt in the Laurentians, I wrote my first poem. And then another and another. It was as if a dam burst, releasing years of pent-up feelings, painful childhood memories, unhealed adolescent wounds, all intermingled with the sharp debris of bereavement, onto page after page of my notebooks.

I wrote about my frustrations on the bench—the human face of law.

Before long I'd accumulated a sizable collection of poems.

My manuscript would have gathered dust in a drawer but for my daughter Mira, who one morning mentioned a poetry workshop by Susan Musgrave, the well-known Canadian poet, to be held at the Lake of Bays in the summer of 1996. Spurred by my children, I decided to go.

Susan generously agreed to read the manuscript. Imagine my surprise the next morning when I heard her say: "We've got to find you a publisher," and even offered to write an introduction. After that, events moved swiftly. Barry Callaghan, the distinguished publisher and poet, to whom Susan had referred me, was equally enthusiastic. My first book of poetry, *Silver Mercies*, came out in 1997. Mary's suicide was an axe breaking the frozen seas within me, and seven more collections, the latest in 2007, rapidly followed.

One pleasant surprise was the positive reaction of my colleagues on the bench. While judges and poets both work with words, for lawyers and judges they are primarily utilitarian, tools to build arguments and render judgments. For poets, words are windows for "intense seeing" as the poet Lorna Crozier put it.

I had worked almost exclusively with the left side of the brain, the seat of logic and common sense. Bounded by technical legal reasoning, knowledge of the law, and the restraints of precedent, I had little room for literary imagination, intuition and emotion. While judges struggle to preserve the "human touch", the reality is they are in the unenviable business of judging others.

In my metamorphosis from judge to "poet-judge", I came to see more clearly that we are all on a common journey toward death, and that all human judgments are at best one-sided and incomplete.

> *"There is a field/ beyond ideas / of right doing and wrong doing/ where the soul/ can lie down among/ wildflowers / and lack nothing........"*

My wife's suicide gave me a chance to see life from the other side of the bench. In a sense I became the judged, the person bearing the weight of guilt and shame. I learned that mercy begins at home, and to forgive one's self is the precondition of compassion for others. Poetry rekindled my commitment as a judge.

By permitting me to "see behind the shutters normally drawn over the human face," as Al Purdy wrote, poetry helped me to connect with others even in the bleak and impersonal Siberia of the courtroom. I began to appreciate more fully what Oliver Wendell Holmes, the eminent American jurist, said: "The life of the law is not logic but experience."

With the passage of time I stopped blaming God, Whom I'd come to believe was only a convenient label we stick onto the random evils that befall us. Gradually I abandoned the death question " why?" and started to ask the life question " what now?" My children were the first to notice a change: I became mellower and more empathetic, they claimed. As a judge, I redoubled my efforts to balance mercy and justice, always a delicate task.

Chinks in our legal system stood out more starkly. I became increasingly disturbed by the exorbitant cost of litigation, and the folly of families squandering the equity in their homes & precious life savings on self-defeating lawsuits. The reality of "pocketbook justice" reinforced my conviction that that the law favours the rich.

Status, power, money
like straw , feathers, dust
are insubstantial things,

but if they all blow one way
that's the way the law bends.

To avoid cynicism, the occupational hazard of judging, I constantly had to remind myself that people are greater and better than they sometimes appear in the distorted mirror of the courtroom.

The plight of others began to reach me deeply. I recall the case of a major bank that sought judgment on a debt against a woman with three small children whose husband had abandoned them after squandering the funds on drugs and gambling. The woman who co-signed the promissory note, lived in a dingy apartment and was struggling to eke out an existence for herself and the children on $25,000 a year as a clerk in a department store, with no support and no savings.

Judges are sworn to follow the law (not their private consciences I knew), but I also knew the law could sometimes be an ass. Though counsel for the bank presented a strong case I dismissed the lawsuit, citing "duress & coercion" in the co-signing of the note. Almost immediately counsel sprang to his feet.

"But your Honour…" he began, but I cut him off.

"You can't squeeze blood from a stone," I barked, "if you don't like my decision, appeal." Alone in chambers afterwards I began to wonder if I wasn't playing God, compensating for His/Her failure to save my wife from the Black Dog.

More and more I sought ways to encourage litigants to settle. One morning a married couple appeared in court, each brandishing a long list of complaints against the other. Though seated only a short distance apart, their stiff posture and averted eyes gave no hint that they even acknowledged the other's presence. Detecting a residue of tenderness in their voices when they spoke of each other, I seized the opportunity to suggest they talk privately in a witness room to see if they could iron out their differences.

At 11 a.m. my court constable said: "I think they're talking."

A half-hour later she returned. "Guess what, I heard them laughing."

At the noon break she entered my chambers, a broad smile on her face: "You won't believe this, your Honour, but they're going out to lunch together." And when court reconvened at 2 p.m., the lawyers rose to announce that the parties had amicably settled all their issues.

Now a judge's job is not a popularity contest. As one wise old jurist said: "With every decision you make a temporary friend and a permanent enemy", but that day I left the courthouse levitating on air, knowing I'd made a small contribution to the Administration of Justice.

One of the most gratifying moments of my years on the bench was a letter I got from a young man I'd sentenced to reformatory. He wrote me how his life had completely turned around, that he planned to get married soon and it was something I'd said to him in court that had made the difference. For days my feet barely touched the ground.

What had I done? Nothing extraordinary except step out of my role as judge for a moment and talk to him as a fellow human being;

...learning
how we are all linked together,
how love can only be broken
one link at a time.

Because poetry is timeless and universal, it also gave me the courage to speak my deepest yearnings and to venture forth toward those invisible angels who feed our hunger for justice.

Bring the clear mirror,
let her see
the jaded eye,
the unforgiving mouth,
let her face break down in tears.

Give back her brown nakedness,
her four , strong limbs,
let her breathe freely,
break softly into new fields.

Ancient Chinese wisdom says it best: poetry is like being alive twice. Poetry gave me a second chance. In a sense, poetry saved my life.

Minutes of the Meeting

Marilyn Gear Pilling

Odile walks. Warren lets the horses out so they can go down to the creek and drink from a small area that is not frozen. Their feet fall through the deep snow crust; it cuts their ankles. He returns them to the barn, sets pails of snow to melt. The day he heard, the electricity went off. Stayed off for three days.

• • •

A persistent east wind blows across Lake Ontario, bringing snow. The heat in this building appears to be off. Coffee and water are available. I accept coffee in a Styrofoam cup from my sister and encircle it with my hands. It's warmth I'm looking for; I will not drink it. Water is all I've taken since yesterday at one thirty-one in the afternoon. The water cooler makes a sucking glug sound, almost like a stomach turning inside out.

This is a meeting, I realize with surprise. We have a Chairperson, who is barely up to the task. He has dressed for the part, in black suit and white shirt. He has groomed himself, dark hair cut short, nails trimmed. There is nothing he can do, this Friday morning in February, about the incisor missing from the middle of his lower jaw. The empty space is prominent as he talks. By the time he has spoken two sentences, it is obvious that he is afraid of us. I don't blame him. His hand trembles, his voice shakes a little. My sister moves to his side.

My sister. Dr. Marie Gear. Mrs. Larry Cerson in private life. She is the helper, the centre of the family, the one to whom we turn in a crisis. Because of the cold,

Marie has kept on her multicoloured scarf. The scarf clashes in texture and in colour with what she's wearing. Our ridiculous human brain, some part of it always busy with matters daily, tiny, even petty, no matter what else is happening.

Also present are those who have been called together to discuss the issues on the agenda and come to decisions. My brother, Warren Gear. My ex sister-in-law, Odile Gaillard Gear. *La belle soeur*, she would be called in her native country of France.

The "children"—ages twenty-eight, twenty-six, twenty-four, twenty-two. The youngest, Stéphanie, age nineteen, is not with us.

Marie, myself and my husband are here to support these, the primary participants.

My *belle-soeur* opens the proceedings with an announcement about her last-born child. Her large dark eyes tilt upwards at the outer corner. She is composed. "Stéphanie is not here, in Georgetown," she says. "She is in Hamilton." She looks at my husband Dan and me as she says this; we live in Hamilton.

"Why… is…she in Hamilton?"

"Because, Merlund, (Odile has always called me Merlund), that is where the coroner is."

"Oh."

"I have just spoken to the coroner." Odile's tone is matter of fact. "Stéphanie's body has no head. There is a left ear; that is all."

Aimée has been crying silently. At this, her sobs become audible, her jittering leg temporarily still. I look at my niece, until yesterday the middle child of five. My tears spill over, run down my cheeks and neck. They are warm. I am grateful for the warmth. This room is like a morgue.

André is sitting on the sofa that his sister Aimée—his only sister, I realize with a start—is standing in front of. He reaches for the Kleenex box, hands one tissue to his sister, one to me. Closest in age to Stéphanie, André worked from home last summer, in order to be near her. Begged her to get better. Protected her. Cajoled her.

Through the ringing of my ears and the muffled thud of the soft drink machine, I hear our Chair say that his name is Jeffery Jordan. He is sorry for our loss. We must decide whether the youngest member of our family will be cremated or whether her body will be buried in a coffin. We must decide whether to have a funeral, whether to have a visitation.

I think of the Tibetans, how they put their dead on the mountaintops and let the birds pick their bones clean. My coat is beside me on the sofa; I pull it over my knees.

André says, "What's a visitation?"

"Before we begin," says Odile. "I would like to say something." She looks at us and speaks with authority. "These decisions belong to the keeds."

All of us have for years called Odile and Warren's children "the keeds," for we find Odile's way of saying the word charming.

These decisions belong to the keeds. My stomach unclenches a little and Marie sits down. Warren and Odile are estranged, in every sense of the word. They cannot be in the same room as a pending decision and not fight about it.

"What's the difference between a visitation and a funeral?" says André.

"Could you disconnect the coke machine?" says my sister. "I can't hear a thing."

Jeffery Jordan jumps to his feet and pulls the plug, then explains to André about visitations and funerals. Marie adds more information. Though I believe that my role at this meeting is to provide silent support, I add that the funeral is a ritual. That rituals are important, that human beings have used them for millennia to help ourselves through milestones such as puberty, marriage, death. That our society has forgotten the importance of ritual.

Having delivered this little lecture, I subside into my coat. The others receive it with tolerant expressions. Stéphanie's father, my brother Warren, is the exception. He turns on me his darkest frown.

The keeds decide quickly to have both visitation and funeral. They decide to have their sister's body cremated; this is what she would have preferred, they say.

Marie stops them at this point: "Are you comfortable with that, Danelle?"

Danelle is the wife of my brother's second son, Maurice. Her face is the white of Sleeping Beauty's in her coffin. Since Christmas, she and Maurice have been giving a home to Stéphanie, who dropped out of university in January.

It is Danelle, age twenty-three, who found Steph's suicide note yesterday morning when she went downstairs to the tiny, windowless, basement room Steph had chosen for herself. She looks up now from between the curtains of chestnut hair that match her eyes. "It's okay," she whispers.

"I know it's against your beliefs," says Marie.

"It wouldn't be okay for my body to be cremated," says Danelle. "It's okay for Steph. She had no religious beliefs."

"Are we going to have Stéphanie's body at the funeral?" says Odile. "What is left of it?"

Maurice says that he and Danelle would prefer to have the body there, for religious reasons. Maurice's face is the same colour as his wife's. Yesterday morning, 02.22.07, a date that will be to our family as 09.11 is to the world, Maurice got up as usual at five a.m., in order to ride the horses at Woodbine. Steph made herself coffee as her brother ate his bowl of oatmeal porridge. When Maurice left his townhouse at five thirty-five, Steph was sipping coffee and watching Seinfeld on her computer.

A week before Steph's death, Maurice had had another conversation with his youngest sister in which he attempted to counter her negative views of the world and herself. This time, frustration ignited the coal that had burned in his gut for the past three years. The fire flashed up his throat and out his mouth: "Why wouldn't you just throw yourself on the tracks, if that's how you feel?"

Ten minutes after Maurice has left for work, Stéphanie walks in the February darkness to the train track. She chooses a spot directly back of her mother's townhouse. She lays her head on the rail and waits for the six-fifteen train.

Three years ago, almost to the day, Maurice happened to stop at his mother's townhouse to pick up a video and found his sister near death, empty pill bottles on the floor. Since that afternoon, a sword has been directly over the heads of Odile, Warren, the keeds. Now the sword has fallen; it has sliced their lives cleanly from meaning, the invisible net that gets you up in the morning and carries you through the days and years.

Aimée shifts her weight from one foot to the other and hugs herself tightly. If the body is there, she says, she can't come inside to the visitation, or the funeral. It's okay, she says, she'll just stay outside.

The oldest, Philippe, suggests a vote.

Again, I break my pact with myself to remain silent: "Aimée's feelings are so intense that she won't be able to be with us if Stéphanie's body is present. Should we maybe consider going with Aimée's wishes rather than voting?"

Immediately, Danelle says that it's more important to have Aimée inside. The others readily agree.

"Steph would have wanted her organs donated," says Maurice.

"Yes," say the others.

"You have to be alive for your organs to be taken," says Marie. "Only the eyes can be donated after you're dead."

"Unfortunately, that will not be possible," says Odile.

"You have to be alive?" says André.

"On life support," says Marie.

Jeffery Jordan says that we need to write Stéphanie's obituary right away, if it's to make the Saturday *Star*. We need to let people know about the funeral.

He asks for the full name of the deceased.

"Stéphanie Marie Gear," says Odile.

My sister, Marie, who is childless, covers her mouth with her scarf and begins to weep silently. Aimée's tears begin again, then mine. The men stare straight ahead, faces ashen. Odile alone looks normally composed. None of this has really happened yet, for her, I realize. She is in shock. Later is when she'll need us, when everyone returns to their lives and she begins to feel the severance work of the sword.

Jordan asks for our names as we wish them to appear in the obituary. He nods at my sister. "Marie Cerson and her husband Larry," she says.

My brother Warren, who so far has not spoken, says, "GEAR." His voice is a sharp report across frigid air. "Marie GEAR," he repeats. I move closer to my husband, cover us both with my winter coat.

So quietly it's hard to hear, Marie says, "It's Cerson."

"So you're not a GEAR anymore?"

I try to keep my brother's many losses in the forefront of my mind and heart as I watch him stare, lip curled, at our sister, the person who has helped him and his family over the years more than anyone in the world. His hair sticks out over his ears and collar. You can smell the barn on his clothes.

Our Chair raises the delicate matter of what container will transport Stéphanie's body from the funeral home to the crematorium. He opens a little book and begins showing coffin-like boxes. This one is a medium price, made of simple wood and with a pillow, he says.

"Stéphanie will not be needing a pillow," says Odile. Again, Aimée's sobs become audible.

"How much does it cost?" says my brother Warren.

"Five hundred dollars," says Jeffery Jordan.

"What happens to the box?" says Warren.

Jeffery Jordan looks at the floor. "It will be…cremated," he says.

"Do you have something cheaper?" says Warren.

Marie crosses her right leg over her left and moves to the edge of her chair. Maurice and Danelle exchange a look.

Jeffery Jordan says they have particle board, simply a box, with no interior. He holds up the picture.

"How much is it?" says Warren.

"Two hundred and fifty dollars," says Jeffery Jordan.

"Don't you have a cardboard box?" says Warren. His voice is loud, with an edge of danger.

Marie shifts in her chair, opens her mouth to speak, closes it.

In a quiet voice, André says, "We don't want cardboard."

"Don't you have a cardboard box?" Warren repeats, his voice louder. His eyes shoot shards at Jeffery Jordan.

André jumps to his feet. "We're not having cardboard."

"It's just going to be burnt," says Warren, to his youngest son. "He turns to Jeffery Jordan. "How much is it? Where's the picture?"

I feel my throat close. The air is so cold it's hard to breathe. I remember André, three years ago, still a teenager: "I could kill my father."

Jeffery Jordan says one hundred and twenty-five dollars and shows the picture without looking at anyone.

"We'll take cardboard," says Warren.

I turn to Danelle, ask her what Steph would have wanted.

Curtains of hair. The white face, the whisper. "Steph was worried about the environment."

The keeds decide that cardboard would be the least damaging to the environment. André sits down. None of them looks at their father.

Jeffery Jordan's bottom teeth look as if they might buckle into the empty space in the middle. He raises his head, looks at Marie. "I'm sorry. I forgot the last item. Where do you wish to bury the ashes?"

We've talked about this, says Philippe. We want the ashes buried in Huron County. It's the only place we have roots, we'll never return to Georgetown. All of us remember summers on the farm with Grandma and Grandpa Gear. We were happy then. We want Steph buried with our grandparents.

I look at my brother. His face is unreadable but a muscle jumps in his cheek. I know that to have his daughter's ashes in his mother and father's plot in Belgrave, six miles from his farm is what he would want, know that on quiet summer afternoons he will go and sit with her by her grave. He and Marie and I will be buried there too, once our blink of life is over.

We agree that Stéphanie's remains will be interred in the spring, when frost has left the ground.

Jeffery Jordan rises to his feet. The meeting is adjourned.

• • •

Odile walks. Sometimes she walks the track. André quits school and goes to Thailand. Aimée quits her job.

Maurice and Danelle sell their townhouse and move to Manitoba. Philippe goes to work as usual. Warren lets the horses out so they can go down to the creek and drink from a small area that is not frozen. Their feet fall through the deep snow crust; it cuts their ankles. He returns the horses to the barn, sets pails of snow to melt. The February day he heard, the electricity went off. Stayed off for three days.

In May, a filly is born to Warren's thoroughbred mare. He names her Stéphanie's Honour. In August, he finds the four month old colt in the back field, the chestnut hair on her front legs and along her left flank badly singed. She has been struck dead by lightning.

My brother goes to bed for a week.

On the eighth day, he gets to his feet, walks unsteadily to the stove and prepares hot mash for the remaining horses. He goes out into the August morning. Calls the horses in from the north field.

6

Seeds of a Bailout

Anna Yin

The chilly wind blows
leaves hastily fall.
In shattered scarlet
trees, young and old
shiver.

On Wall Street
behind bleeding screens
reddish clumps
become burning fires.

Among branches' shadowy limbs
woodpeckers retreat
their black beaks blunt.

Hollow eyes stare at the panicked street:
lies tangle in greed climb the twisted charts.

Soon, it all will turn to ash
inhaled by everyone—
wring sweat and blood
from our flesh.

Plowing through billions of seeds
we hold our breath—
with the coming snow
what else but plowing?

“This is your goodbye kiss, Bush, you dog!”

Roger Bell

Wipe off their self-satisfied smirks.

Hurl your work boots

at the sheiks who build eye-blue lakes in the thirsty deserts
and on them float islands of petroleum glitz,
raise unto the heavens monuments to hubris;

and at the grey-suited moguls in Calgary boardrooms
who torture filthy confessions from reluctant sands
and would drill the wilderness full of oozing wounds.

Pitch your stiletto heels

at the artisans of war
who make landmines by day in windowless rooms
and by night read bedtime stories to their ingenuous children

at the merchants of death who peddle AK47s to Mugabe
and fill forests with missiles as angry as denuded trees,
as fingers pointing at the stars in accusation.

Sling your well-worn sandals

at the jackals who strap themselves in glory,
who immolate, then soothe their souls at fountains

of the blood of others interrupted going about their daily business

at they who hold their holy books high as if
to proclaim their virtue and
to overshadow the brightest lights of love.

Heave your evening slippers

at the manipulators of figures
the magicians who reap bonuses in the high millions
while their workers gnaw fatigue and resignation

at the politicians who seep sympathy
and weep copious camera-caught tears at children in poverty
then leave in limos for fundraisers and four-course dinners.

Rise up and toss your footwear
in the faces of these curs
then go forever after barefoot in the tender soil of forgiveness
feel the true and humble earth between your toes.
There is still hope for the innocent skin
that unshod steps towards salvation.

Who Knew

Ed Woods

bailouts (Enron)
who saw (Enron) it coming
how did (Enron) it happen
where was (Enron) the IRS
stock market (Enron) stability
Arthur Anderson (Enron) fudging
it came (Enron) out of nowhere

and the (Enron) perpetrators
sleep well each (Enron) night

Homeless

Ed Woods

the toughest part
of being homeless
is choosing
what area of the pavement
will be your bed tonight

Fail

Ed Woods

I must cheat
to be successful

hard work and toil
paying continuous
bills and taxes
plagues the masses

corporations squander
cheat to win big
pensions and stock options
cashed in a the right time

I feel proud for contributing
the bankrupt money
for their bailout solution

Greed

Ed Woods

I cannot stop thinking
about greed
corporate greed
individual greed
my own stupidity over greed

money alone drives this world
of shareholding vultures

I picture the demised
reaching back from a grave
not to touch a spouse's hand
for that would involve a soul
or human emotions
remote from their existence

they want to touch a dollar
the feel of splendid paper
view envious numeration
and glance upon stock quotes

precious dollars
gouged or stolen
forced or traded
coerced or foreclosed
it doesn't matter
it's the same feeling

grasping a dollar bill
everything in life is good
everything in life is proper

Acknowledgements

"To Be Creative" by Margaret Atwood appeared in *The Globe & Mail*, and *The Writers' Union of Canada Newsletter*, and is reprinted here by permission of the author.

"Labour" is previously published in *Something More Miraculous*, Oberon Press, 2004 and appears here with the permission of the author.

The lyric "Crow Filled Sky" appeared originally in the eponymous CD, *Crow Filled Sky*, and is reprinted here with permission of the author, Michael Schatte.

"The Man Who Made Hope" appeared originally in the anthology *"Cuba, Si"* (Hidden Brook Press, 2010) and in the book, *Dressed in Dead Uncles*, (Black Moss Press, 2010). It is reprinted here with permission of the author.

Author Bios

Margaret Atwood is an internationally-acclaimed author. A recipient of many prestigious awards for her work, she is one of the most important writers living in Canada.

Mike Beauchamps is an urban photographer from Windsor, Ontario, whose work has appeared in other titles by Black Moss Press.

Roger Bell's most recent book is *You Tell Me.* In 2011 Black Moss Press will publish his memoir, *A Smaller Time.*

James Clarke, a retired Ontario Superior Court Judge, is the author of two prose and eight books of poetry (Exile Editions). He lives in Guelph Ontario.

Antony Di Nardo's poetry has appeared in journals across Canada and internationally. He also writes fiction and nonfiction. He lives in Beruit where he teaches at International College.

Chris Faiers was the recipient of the inaugural Milton Acorn Memorial People's Poetry Award. He is a people's poet living in Ontario.

Marty Gervais is a writer and photographer from Windsor, Ontario.

Richard (Tai) Grove is the publishing editor of Hidden Brook Press. Founding president of the Canada Cuba Literary Alliance, he is a widely published poet and author.

Don Gutteridge is the author of more than thirty books. He is professor emeritus in the Faculty of Education, The University of Western Ontario.

Andrew Johnson is a Hamilton, Ontario-based writer and editor. His latest project is a group of poems called Poems for the 7-11 at College and Spadina.

Shane Joseph is the author of two novels and a collection of short stories. His work has appeared in Canada, the UK, the USA, India and Sri Lanka.

Dylan Lee currently teaches English in Korea where he lives with his wife and son.

John B. Lee is the author of over fifty published books. Recent titles include *Dressed in Dead Uncles*, (Black Moss Press, 2010) and *Sweet Cuba*, (Hidden Brook Press, 2010).

Bernice Lever, Bowen Island, BC, is a poet and editor; ran WAVES '72-'87; and latest book is *Generation* (Black Moss Press, 2009).

Jennifer McMullan is a Windsor-based writer and graduate of the University of Windsor.

R.D. Roy is the author of a novella, several books of poetry, and 2 collections of short stories. He lives in Trenton, Ontario.

Michael Schatte is a singer, songwriter musician-extraordinaire with several CDs to his credit. His most recent CD *Crow Filled Sky* features fifteen original songs.

Eric Solomon is professor emeritus at San Francisco State University. His literary criticism has appeared widely in the United States. A baseball enthusiast, he lives in San Francisco.

Sarah St. Pierre is a photographer from Peterborough, Ontario.

Robert Earl Stewart's collection *Something Burned Along the Southern Border* (Mansfield Press) was shortlisted for the Gerald Lampert Memorial Award. He lives in Windsor.

Robert Sward is an author of over thirty books. He has taught at Cornell University, the Iowa Writers' Workshop, and UC Santa Cruz. He lives in Santa Cruz, California.

Duane Tucker is a screenwriter, critic, essayist and poet. In a previous incarnation he appeared in over 40 films and TV shows.

Sheila Tucker only recently began submitting poetry and, to her delight, has won prizes and been published in several anthologies.

John Wing is a standup comedian and writer. Born in Sarnia, he lives in Sunland, California

Ed Woods is a Dundas Ontario creative writer of life events and experiences or observations classed as Industrial Poetry.

Anna Yin won 2010 MARTY Award and 2005 Ted Plantos Memorial Award. Her works were in a Canadian Studies' textbook used by Humber College.